# POWER
## PRESENTATIONS

### How to
### Connect with Your Audience
### and Sell Your Ideas

Marjorie Brody

Shawn Kent

John Wiley & Sons, Inc.
New York • Chichester • Brisbane • Toronto • Singapore

In recognition of the importance of preserving what has been
written, it is a policy of John Wiley & Sons, Inc., to have
books of enduring value published in the United States
printed on acid-free paper, and we exert our best efforts
to that end.

### *Library of Congress Cataloging-in-Publication Data*

Brody, Marjorie
    Power presentations : how to connect with your audience and sell
your ideas / by Marjorie Brody ; Shawn Kent.
      p. cm.
    Includes bibliographical references and index.
    ISBN 0-471-55960-1 (cloth). —ISBN 0-471-55961-X (paper)
    1. Business presentations.  2. Business communication.  I. Kent,
Shawn.  II. Title.
HF5718.22.B75   1992
658.4'52—dc20                        92-10949

Printed in the United States of America

10 9 8

To Our Families

# ACKNOWLEDGMENTS

Many people have influenced us in positive ways. We are mindful of Albert Einstein's wisdom: "A hundred times each day, I remind myself that my inner and outer lives are dependent upon the labors of other (people), living and dead, and that I must exert myself in order to give in the same measure as I have received and am still receiving." There are so many people to thank.

If you have been in one of our audiences, training programs, or consulting sessions, we thank you. Your feedback helped us to create this book.

We would like to acknowledge all our corporate clients who shared their experiences with us, and our families who encouraged us to share our techniques and ideas. Thanks also to Jeff Davidson for coaching us to find the best possible publisher, and to John Mahaney of John Wiley & Sons, Inc., who had faith in us.

M.B. and S.K.

Thanks to my parents for their high expectations.

Special thanks to Alan for encouraging me through my mid-life crisis and the changes that ensued. Also thanks to my children, Amy and Julie, for being who they are and for their love.

Thanks to all Brody Communication associates and staff who support me on a daily basis.

M.B.

Thanks to Elizabeth Jeffries for being my role model and dear friend.

Thanks to Rick Semetti; your encouragement helped me to pursue this project.

Thanks to Evan Hanby, Cindy Roney, Lydia Young, and Marilyn Muchnick, for their friendship which I value so much.

For the unique support given to me by Mary Egan, Steve Miller, and Greg Minor. I am grateful. Thanks to all my friends and associates at IMS America.

S.K.

# CONTENTS

# INTRODUCTION

**W**ould you like to know the single most important element of an effective presentation? It's the ability to *connect with your audience; it's showing the audience what's in it for them.* Think of it—without an audience you literally have no one to listen to you.

## WHY YOU NEED THIS BOOK

Although other books on public speaking focus primarily on the speaker, we've learned, in working with thousands of executives in hundreds of organizations, that effective speaking is an *audience-centered* sport. The most effective speakers never lose this focus. By following the audience-centered advice and information provided in this book, you'll gain many benefits, including:

- *A Greater Sense of Personal Confidence.* After successfully speaking to groups, your interpersonal speaking skills will rise dramatically. A key ingredient to a powerful presentation is the confidence that you exude. Confidence comes from preparation, adequate practice, and literally, knowing who is in the audience. You'll know what you want to say, to whom, and how you want to say it.

- *The Ability to Speak to a Wide Range of Groups in Different Settings.* You need not fear speaking in an unfamiliar environment. We'll give you techniques for communicating effectively with a wide variety of audiences.

- *Enhanced Opportunities for Career Advancement and Promotion.* We've found that learning and using polished speaking skills will get you promoted faster than any other skill.

In addition, after reading this book, you'll be better able to:

- Organize presentations to achieve your purpose.
- Use factual, logical, and captivating supporting materials.
- Use visuals and audiovisual equipment.
- Add nonverbal power to your presentation.
- Answer questions effectively.

Preparing for a presentation is a learned skill. What is the best way to learn that skill? We took the mystery out of putting together a presentation by addressing each step involved. You'll know how to connect with audiences after practicing the activities we suggest. This book goes beyond Speech Class 101. Once you have learned the basics, you'll begin to master the art of presenting.

People often ask us for a videotape of the right way to give a presentation. "Is there one right way to make a presentation?" we hear. Every audience is different, and thus every presentation may need to be. Also, since we all have different strengths, there is *no one right way for everyone.* Speakers who know their audiences and communicate with them in a manner that holds attention, encounter success again and again.

## *HOW DO YOU FIT INTO A PRESENTATION?*

Any presentation creates a triangular relationship of the speaker, the audience, and the presentation itself. You have knowledge, information, or services that an audience wants. Your goal is to provide information effectively to that audience. All decisions related to speaking—your purpose, kinds of supporting data, method of organization, use of visuals, and style of delivery are *based on the needs and interests of the audience.*

In any communication, be it with one or a number of people—selling, training, or speaking—there are always three components: speaker or presenter, information, and audience. At the top of the triangle is the presenter whose role is to communicate to the audience who came to hear the information. The presenter is the vehicle through which the message is delivered to the audience. The presenter's task is to join the bottom two corners of the triangle; the audience and the information must connect for the triangle to be complete. In most presentations, the audience came to hear the information.

Unless the speaker is very famous, the audience is listening to connect with the information—not the speaker. We might listen to George Bush, Barbara Walters, or Ted Koppel because of who they are, not because of what we want to learn or know from them.

In most instances it is the message that is important.

## HOW WILL USING THIS BOOK HELP YOU ADVANCE?

We've structured this book so that by the time you finish reading it and following the simple, practical steps suggested in each chapter, you will be able to give a presentation that will win respect and enhance your credibility with your audience.

To be a professional means to accept responsibility for both actions and results. It is to act in the best interests of those served, to help them grow rather than stagnate. When we accept the responsibility for professionally influencing the lives and actions of other people, we need to do all we can to make that influence as successful and positive as possible.

Your presentation won't, indeed can't, be effective if you are communicating at the wrong level for your audience. To inform, persuade, or entertain requires understanding the needs and desires of the people sitting in front of you—your audience. The challenge is to read your audience constantly and be flexible enough to vary your approach if you are losing their attention.

Before you listen to a speaker or buy a product, you ask yourself, "What's in It for Me?" (WIIFM). Likewise, your audience will be asking themselves, "What's in It for Me?" As a speaker, you'll want to address your presentation to this question, "What's in It for Them?" (WIIFT). Your goal is to focus on your audience, not yourself, and to keep in mind that speaking is an audience-centered sport. Once you know the components of a sport, you use them each time you play. For example, if you were playing golf, you would need to know the proper stance, grip for your clubs, the approach, the swing, and the follow-through. In learning the sport, you'll break each of those steps down into component parts to become accomplished at each individually. Then you will begin to put the components back together to play the game. Mastering speaking is like mastering any sport. Each component requires practice. For example, for delivery techniques, eye communication is going to require specific practice. You may naturally be good at eye communication but have trouble gesturing effectively. You will have to practice gestures making sure you coordinate the gestures with your eye communication.

Presenting is a matter of developing techniques that are comfortable for you, that are consistent with your message, and most importantly that will work for your audience. For example, if you are speaking to a group of technical quality control managers or very analytical groups, you'll need to modify your behavior to appeal to that group. With analytical or introverted groups, you will pull in your gestures, tone, and animation; speak slower; and give plenty of factual details. On the other hand, when presenting to marketing, sales, and extroverted groups, you'll need to be more animated, speak louder and faster, and be lighter in technical details.

You also need to be aware of the region or culture in which you are presenting. If you are in the southern part of the United States, you'll need to slow your pace; if you speak too quickly, you will lose your rapport with your audience. In the Northeast, you'd need to speak faster to be taken seriously.

Senior management usually does not want as many details in the presentation; such managers want bottom-line facts and how you got there. You'll need the details for the question-and-answer session that follows but do not "data dump" in the presentation. The underpinnings, step-by-step "how to's" do not belong in a high-level presentation. This group also will prefer visual aids that show graphically how the parts fit together—pie charts, for example. The analytical or technical supervisors and technicians will expect the raw data—a simple pie chart will not give them enough.

In the United States, we tend to expect direct eye contact as we speak. Yet there are other cultures who are shy or reticent, preferring not to look directly into another's eyes. Auditorially dominant thinkers often do not maintain direct eye contact because they are processing their thoughts by looking down. Some Asian audiences most likely would not like direct eye contact because looking directly into someone's eyes is considered to be poor manners. The more we know about our audience, the more we can be flexible and adapt our delivery style, organization of materials, and the data that we use.

Again, there is no one right way. The key is to adapt your presentation to your audience: How much data you give, types of material to use, references, visual aids, structure, and delivery techniques will depend on to whom you are presenting. Every detail about the audience will enable you to better tailor your presentation to your audience's needs.

Whenever we are presenting, we are sharing our thoughts, opinions, and ideas; we are asking others to buy into them. We are persuading others to continue listening to us and to accept what we've said. The consequence to this responsibility is that we must take the time to prepare appropriate presentations. If you do not analyze your audience properly, you will not give them the information they need. You might turn them off, offend them, be too sketchy or detailed. We are accountable for what we do in every area of our lives—each presentation counts. Everything is connected. When we give our ideas, we will impact the audience—intentionally or unintentionally, effectively or ineffectively.

Successful presenters have prepared themselves so well that they can customize their material as needed to fit the audience. Use your audience's language: Know their theme and their needs, state these up front in your presentation. Connect with your audience before you begin to delve into details. Influence your audience by design. When you do, you'll have to know your own presentation materials so well that you can flex your style to suit the audience. If you realize what you are doing is not working and you know your subject, you will be able to make a modification in your delivery to meet the audience's need without losing the group: the better prepared, the more flexibility. This does *not* mean "canned." Prepared means ownership or control of material and gives you the ability to make any changes necessary depending on the situation, timing, and people.

## HOW TO USE THIS BOOK

We begin by discussing the excitement all speakers feel before going on stage (what some people call stage fright) and how to make that excitement work in your favor. Then we examine nonverbal aspects of speaking, steps in preparing your presentation, informative and persuasive speaking, impromptu speaking, and helpful hints about aspects that affect your presentation.

Review the whole book quickly to familiarize yourself with the general range of material, scan the Contents, and highlight the chapters that most interest you. Read them first.

When you are ready to prepare your next presentation, read Part Four, "Communicating on Purpose." This will give you clarity on your intention. Do Part Two, "Groundwork," next so you have the initial preparations underway. Then read Part Three, "Working on the Presentation." To acquire technical skills, read Part Five, "Mastering the Mechanics;" and to gain confidence and self-control, study Part One, "Taking Control." Use the Checklists to double-check your preparation.

For ease of presentation, we've used the pronoun "I," though the information and suggestions may be from either or both of us. Also, we have used both "she" and "he" in examples throughout the text to avoid any gender bias. Unless otherwise noted, all information in this book applies equally to men and women.

P
A
R
T

O
N
E

# TAKING
# CONTROL

## WHAT'S IN IT FOR YOU

Being in control helps us to feel better
when we present. Overall if we "own" the
material, the situation, and the meeting
room, we are able to be flexible in how we
communicate with others. Chapter 1 will
show you how to turn stage fright into excitement so you can give the best possible
presentation. Being able to prepare for
stage fright and convert it to excitement
will change the way you feel about the
idea of giving a presentation. *The New Eng-
land Journal of Medicine* says that giving a

presentation is as stressful as taking a stress test. After reading Chapter 1, you will make use of positive stress to help you give presentations with energy and excitement.

Chapter 2 will show you exercises to use before you present to help you warm up. In any sport, you need to have your body limbered up. Here you'll learn how to limber up for the presentation, that is, to stretch your body and vocal cords so you are not tight. If we see a speaker who is tense, we know it and become tight just watching. Look loose and relaxed and *be* loose and relaxed by warming up.

Nonverbal signals such as what you wear, your facial expressions, and the pitch, volume, and pace of your voice will influence your listener more than the words you use. In your delivery, you must be aware of your nonverbal communications. Face to face, people tune into nonverbal signals before they hear one word the speaker says. In Chapter 3, you will learn all the components of nonverbal signals and the tips and techniques to make them consistent with your verbal message.

Chapter 4 discusses gestures. Our gestures need to be connected to our message. A presenter whose gestures are close to the body, tight, and ineffective cannot communicate in an open way that pulls in the audience. Gestures can say more than the words themselves. One way to get more energy from the audience is to use gestures that communicate clearly. Some of us naturally gesture well without awareness that we are competent. If you are comfortable using appropriate gestures, your verbal message will have more impact. You'll learn all the do's and don't's in Chapter Four.

Chapter 5 will teach you how to stay in control. Think of the last time you had a dinner party. You did all the preparation to have a beautiful dinner on the table when the guests arrived. You double-checked the table setting. You pretasted all the dishes served. The flowers were perfect. If you had not prepared the meal with your audience in mind—your guests—you might have run into some trouble. If you prepared the perfect roast beef dinner, with a chicken soup starter and a rich delicious cheesecake for dessert, you may have discovered one of your guests is diabetic, another a vegetarian. It does not matter how well the table is set or how carefully the roast or cake is prepared if the meal is not appropriate for the guests. When you do the groundwork for a presentation, you'll need to learn about your audience to prepare for them. You will learn what to drink and when, why you should bite your tongue, and how to handle an absorbing problem. This chapter even shares what to pack for personal emergencies. You'll stay in control when you are properly prepared. If you *know* that you really know your material, you'll stay cool throughout the presentation.

# 1

## TURNING STAGE FRIGHT INTO EXCITEMENT

*Do not be too timid and*
*squeamish about your*
*actions. All life is an*
*experiment.*
    *—Ralph Waldo Emerson*

Nervous about speaking? You are not alone! Surveys indicate that one of the greatest fears people have is a fear of speaking in public. Ranking ahead of fear of death, flying, heights, snakes, and many others, the number one fear cited in survey after survey is the fear of public speaking. In other words, *people would rather die than give a speech!* Whether you are speaking in front of 5 or 500 people, speaking can be a potentially terrifying experience— but it need not be. You can "unlearn" the fear of public speaking by learning the skills to speak in public and feel great about your accomplishments.

Since I give seminar presentations almost every day, people assume that I always feel calm when I start speaking—an incorrect assumption. Can you recall the last time you "performed" in public? Whether the performance was in a music recital, a play, or a sport, you were excited when you began, weren't you? And that's ok; what football coach would want the team members calm when the whistle blows?

I get concerned when I don't feel a little jittery before a presentation. The energy, or anxiety, from excitement is useful. The key is to turn it into a tool to aid you *before* you make the presentation.

> Instead of labeling your pounding heart, sweaty palms, difficult breathing, and upset stomach *stage fright*, try renaming it *excitement*.

To do that conclusively, however, you need first to examine what you are afraid of, check the reality of each fear, and learn skills to keep the fear from becoming destructive.

## WHAT ARE YOU AFRAID OF?

Many a stirring speech has called people to action. President Franklin D. Roosevelt's famous line in his radio address to the nation: "The only thing we have to fear is fear itself." continues to be quoted. As Roosevelt expressed so well, fear can be debilitating. It can keep you from giving your best presentation when you speak in public. The vital information you want to share or the benefits of a new product you are selling can be lost in the nervous shuffle of papers in front of a group. Let's examine four common fears of speakers:

### Fainting

A formal wedding is a perfect example of a potentially nerve-racking event. To get anxious about the big day, you have only to think of the costs involved, the many preparations that may go wrong, and the number of people attending.

Imagine you are getting married. Soon enough, the music starts, and you find yourself walking down the aisle in restrictive, formal wear. You're about to commit to the biggest decision of your life. Short of divorce, the only thing that will part you from your new spouse is death. The music is pounding in your ears. Before you can take your betrothed's hand and try to speak, you've fainted on the floor.

How many times have you actually seen or heard of someone fainting while at the altar? Probably never. Now consider the experience of giving a speech. There is much less at stake in giving a presentation than in getting married, and most of us make it through the marriage ceremony just fine.

One of my students told me how she had fantasized fainting at the beginning of her speech as a foolproof way to avoid giving the speech. Throughout 26 years of teaching speaking skills and giving presentations, I actually have seen only one person faint. This collapse, I later discovered, was caused by low blood sugar and had no direct connection with anxiety. As we'll explore shortly, you can learn to turn prespeech anxiety into productive energy.

## Boring Your Audience

A second common fear speakers share is delivering a presentation that bores the audience. If you approach speaking as an audience-centered sport, you will seldom need to be concerned with boring your audience.

Examine what you are telling your audience to be sure that:

- You are giving them useful information geared to their level of knowledge.

- You have chosen material that is of interest to them and backed it with facts, figures and anecdotes that enhance and illustrate your points.

- You are speaking directly to each and every one of them so there is no reason for them to be bored.

Some people fear that their voice is boring or monotonic. If you approach your presentation with the attitude, "My topic is boring," you'll probably be right. Your goal is to live, act, and generate enthusiasm. You know that you are not going to speak in a monotone on purpose. Simply being aware of your fear will help keep it from happening. By working on personal speaking style skills (described in Chapter 6), you can keep yourself from becoming monotonic in your delivery and increase your chances of being well received.

## Drawing a Blank

You might be afraid of drawing a blank. Unlike fainting, this fear does turn into reality occasionally. You'll want to learn how to "cover for it" when it does. I've seen it happen to a television news anchor. He was unaccustomed to working on remote without a teleprompter. Amid the street noise of traffic and people, he suddenly went blank in mid-sentence.

He was in a terrible position, but he saved the day by frankly admitting that he had gone blank, switching to a different train of thought, and continuing on with his discussion. His good-natured honesty in the situation helped ease the way for those who were watching.

If you draw a blank, simply pause, look at your notes or outline and try to pick it up again, or move on to your next thought in your presentation. Don't be afraid of using your notes to help you get back on track. Continue without apologizing for the small glitch in your speech. Your apology will only focus people's attention and increase awareness of the distraction.

The same advice holds true for making a mistake—my own worst fear when giving a presentation. What if I say something that is not true? Do I let it slide and hope no one notices, or do I call attention to it by correcting it immediately? Of course, a large part of that decision is based on the kind of mistake it is.

When President Bush told a military audience that Pearl Harbor was attacked on September 7th, 1941 (instead of December), he could have used humor to correct the mistake as soon as he recognized it. Always consider the mistake from the point of view of those in the audience. If it has no impact on the audience, I say forget it and plunge on ahead.

### Being Judged by the Audience

Another frequent cause for anxiety is the fear of being judged. We've all judged speakers who have straggly hair, gesture too much, or repeat the same word again and again and again. This makes us even more afraid that when it is our turn to speak, others will scrutinize and condemn us. Yet, we are much harder on ourselves than others will be.

If you are prepared and have practiced your presentation, everything you are responsible for will go smoothly. If you enjoy your subject and truly communicate with the people you are addressing, they will soon forget about, or at least forgive, the napkin still tucked in your waistband.

## GOOD STRESS VERSUS BAD STRESS

Stress has been a recurring topic in the media in recent years. Newspaper and magazine articles warn of the dangers of stress. Millions of dollars are spent by people trying to decrease the stress in their lives. Some of us are so busy trying to stifle stress that we forget some stress is good and can be used to our advantage.

According to Hans Selye, Nobel prizewinner and author of *Stress Without Dis-Stress*, stress is not caused by something within the body but rather by the way we think about what is happening to us. If we *perceive* an event as stressful, difficult, or painful, then it will be. If we tell ourselves that what we are experiencing is exciting, an opportunity, or fun, then it will be.

Stress is our body's reaction to a potential threat. It allows our bodies to get ready to fight or run away from a danger. Stress releases the adrenalin that helps pump more oxygen to our muscles when we are about to start a race, or to the brain when we are about to perform CPR on a drowning victim.

You feel adrenalin pumping into your system before walking on stage or up to a podium. The stress that you are going to learn to handle through relaxation and other skills we'll introduce is the stress that comes from saying, "I can't do this," or "I'm going to fail." I have learned to welcome the nervousness or stress I feel before making a presentation and put it to good use during my seminar presentations, especially presentations on stage fright.

## Surviving the Ordeal of Being on Camera

I knew a corporate communications manager who took a television production course at a state university as part of an executive training program. Class projects included learning how a studio operates and having each student conduct a five-minute interview on camera. This woman, who otherwise was self-assured when speaking before groups of all sizes, was petrified at the thought of being videotaped while everyone watched her on television monitors.

She realized, though, that she could not receive certification if she dropped out and that this part of the training was significant. Since in her position, she was likely to appear on television one day, she relented and prepared for the worst. After all, what was five minutes out of her life?

On the day of the interview, the woman and a classmate were seated on the set with two cameras pointed at them. Suddenly the red light flashed on the top of one camera and the floor manager cued her. She was on the air!

She quickly introduced herself and her "guest" and whizzed through the first five of her questions in only one minute. Four minutes and just five questions to go! With that red light on, each second seemed to last a week. The spotlight was relentless in its glare, and the many eyes staring at the monitors were unmerciful in their inspection of her.

Thankfully, the guest gave a long response to her next question. She was forced to cut him short when the floor manager signaled that the five minutes were almost up. The red light went off, and she was able to leave the hot seat. *She survived*.

This same woman went on to become a writer/producer at a television station. No doubt, her experience on both sides of the camera helped her. Nevertheless, a few simple tips on managing fear could have benefited her greatly. Here are several methods for handling these fears.

*Realize That Anxiety Is Normal.*   Many people feel stage fright before giving a speech. Bob Hope, in spite of his many years on television, says he still gets nervous before going on the air. It is a common occurrence.

Alternatively, have you ever walked to the front of the room to make a presentation and felt utterly calm? Do you think you're going to give a good speech? Coaches don't want their players to be calm before a game. They want them to be energetic and eager to connect.

You want that adrenalin and energy. Tell yourself, "This is not fear. This is excitement." Realize that fear or stage fright is normal, and when you feel your heart pumping, think, "I welcome this, because it means I'm going to perform with more energy. I'm excited to be here." You owe it to your audience to give your peak performance.

*Observe Others.*   Watch the breakfast speaker at Rotary, the President at a press conference, or a manager lead a staff meeting. Study the speakers you encounter and ask yourself what these people are doing that works and what doesn't work.

Make it a practice to observe speaking techniques and how they are being used by the speakers you encounter. Ask yourself which techniques you would like to practice and incorporate into your own presentations.

*Be Aware of Your Own Strengths and Weaknesses.*   None of us are born speakers. We all acquire our skills along the way. To assess your strengths and weaknesses, start by being aware of yourself when you speak, from your style of dress and the way you stand, to the methods that you use to make your point. Discover what your strengths are and play them up. Decide what you can change, and do so. Figure out how to compensate for the things you can't change.

I was faced with the clarity of my strengths and blind spots the first time I took a personality indicator. There are many of these available; most management consultants or training organizations can administer one for you. Knowing my strengths and blind spots has enabled me to put myself into situations that require my strengths—thus I am more valued as a contributor. If I find I am working in a situation that requires my weaknesses to get the job done, I need to be responsible to my own talents and put myself somewhere else that utilizes my strengths. Depending on your personal style, you will deliver your speeches based on your own strengths. Don't let anyone take your personal style from you— it's your greatest asset.

Appearing youthful can work for or against you depending on the ages and skill levels of people in the audience and on your subject matter. If the audience is considerably younger or older than the speaker, she will have to work harder at establishing the relevance of the subject to the audience. When the subject is technical rather than subjective, age matters less to the audience.

While age and other factors, such as personality type and physical appearance, are constants, you can compensate by developing and accenting strengths that counteract the factors that could distance you from an audience.

*Speak Frequently.*   When Franklin D. Roosevelt became President, he relied on his wife, Eleanor, to travel across the country and serve as his fingers on the pulse of the nation. Eleanor had never spoken in public, even when Roosevelt was Governor of New York. Now she had to learn, and learn she did.

Although her first speeches were awkward, through continual practice Eleanor polished her presentation skills over the course of her husband's presidency.

After the death of her husband, she continued her public career, speaking to the United Nations on behalf of war refugees. It was Mrs. Roosevelt's eloquence that made it possible for World War II refugees to stay in their adopted lands rather than being forced to return to the countries that had oppressed them.

If you are not giving presentations on a regular basis, then seek out more opportunities to do so. In the same way that a professional athlete would not expect to win games with only a monthly or bi-monthly practice, you cannot expect to give your peak performance in delivering a speech without regular practice.

You can easily find opportunities to speak where you live and work. Speak at a civic meeting or represent your neighborhood before the city council, volunteer to lecture for the American Red Cross, or become the chairperson for a committee. The more you exercise and flex your presentation skills, the better you will become.

*Prepare and Practice, Practice, Practice.* The first part of preparing is to become a subject matter expert. Then organize your material so it is audience-centered. The audience has to be able to understand the importance of your subject to them. Then practice, practice, practice.

Each time you speak, prepare an outline of the major points and use it to practice the presentation over and over. The outline will be especially useful if you ever draw a blank while speaking.

Another helpful preparation technique is to say the speech differently every time. If you say the same words repeatedly, they become crutches. Then if you get caught up in the rhythm of the words and your mind goes blank, you could really be stuck. It doesn't matter that the words you use or their order are different, the information is the same.

If your presentation is technical or complicated, deliver it first to your spouse or a friend who is most like your intended audience to gauge how easily your material can be understood.

Practice your speech in the same manner that you will be delivering the speech. For example, if you are going to be standing at a podium, stand up when you practice. Tape-record your speech after you have practiced it three times out loud. As you listen to your speech, ask yourself the very important question: If I were a member of this audience would I like the presentation? If so, practice it again, at least three to six times. If not, make the necessary changes and practice, practice, practice.

Having a speech in your head and delivering it are two separate things, as many of us have learned the hard way. A short circuit often occurs between a thought and its expression. Practicing out loud will ensure that the proper connection is made.

After at least three practice runs, arrange your living room or office like the meeting room where you'll be speaking. Talk to the empty chairs and familiarize yourself with gesturing and walking. Practice with any audiovisual equipment you may be using, or if you are going to use a chart and marker, then actually go through the process of writing down your key points as you talk.

If possible, predeliver your speech in the room where you'll be giving it. After your third practice run, go ahead, audio- or videotape yourself. If you are satisfied with how you sound on tape and the evenness of your gestures and motions, then you're ready for an audience. If you aren't satisfied, continue practicing until you are.

When you do deliver your presentation before an audience, approach them as if making this presentation for the first time. Remain interested in the content yourself and be flexible about its presentation. A canned presentation locks you into a speech mode rather than a *heightened conversational mode.* A heightened conversational mode gives you the flexibility to modify your talk to fit the needs of the audience. After all, *their needs* are your reason for being there in the first place.

Let's turn now to Chapter 2 to explore the physical aspects of your preparation to speak.

# 2

# *WARMING UP*

*Sow an act and you reap a habit.*
—*George D. Boardman*

You wouldn't think of doing an hour of aerobics or weightlifting without first warming up and stretching your body, would you? Likewise, you'll want to consider a basic routine of body warm-ups, as a crucial and regular part of your presentation, to help you relax before you speak.

After reading this chapter, if you still don't think body warm-ups are important, try this test: Practice your speech and record it on tape once without warm-up, and then tape it again—after warm-up. Listen to the two recorded speeches. I promise you, the difference will be dramatic.

## THE BASIC ROUTINE

This basic routine can be done in an office or other semi-private place right before the event at which you are giving your presentation.

### Body Warm-Up 1: Rag Doll

Stand up straight with your feet apart in a comfortable balance. Stretch up tall, then bend over by collapsing quickly and loosely

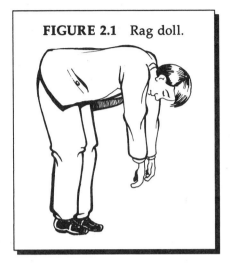

**FIGURE 2.1**  Rag doll.

from the waist with your relaxed arms and hands dangling to the floor. Keep your arms, hands, and neck relaxed so that you look like a rag doll. Do not bounce. Although many of us grew up thinking it was correct to bounce, sports medicine specialists and doctors now say this will hurt your back. After a few seconds, slowly rise up to a straight position, keeping relaxed (see Figure 2.1). Repeat this warm-up several times.

### Body Warm-Up 2: Head Roll

**FIGURE 2.2**  Head roll.

Do this warm-up immediately after the rag doll exercise, while your neck is still relaxed. Stand straight with your hands close to the chest. Begin slowly to rotate your neck, first to the left, then forward with your chin down in front, then to the right (see Figure 2.2). Once again, you will have to break yourself of a habit you may have grown up with: rolling your neck back. This too has recently been found to be unhealthy. Reverse the rotation: right, front, left, front. Be sure to keep your neck relaxed and let your head roll like a dead weight in a socket.

**FIGURE 2.3** Arm swing.

## Body Warm-Up 3: *Arm Swing*

Do this warm-up immediately after the head roll, while your arms are still relaxed. Stand straight with your arms to your sides. Swing your left arm in a large circle from front to back, as if you were doing the back stroke in a swimming pool. Swing your right arm in a large circle from front to back in the same manner.

Reverse and swing your left arm in a large circle from back to front. Do the same with your right arm. Swing your arms in this manner several times (see Figure 2.3).

**FIGURE 2.4** Shoulder shrug.

## Body Warm-Up 4: *Shoulder Shrug*

Do this warm-up next, while your shoulders are still limbered up. Stand straight with your arms to your sides. Using your arms, move your shoulders straight up to the level of your ears. Drop your shoulders back down to their resting position. Shrug your shoulders two more times (see Figure 2.4).

**FIGURE 2.5**   Yawn.

## Body Warm-Up 5: Yawn

If you have done the rag doll and head roll warm-ups correctly, your face and neck muscles and vocal chords will be completely relaxed. Now, standing straight, slowly yawn, sounding an "ahhhhh" on exhalation from the yawn (see Figure 2.5). The sound you make is a relaxed sound. Strive for this relaxation and open quality of the throat whenever you speak.

## Body Warm-Up 6: Abdominal Breathing

Sit upright in a chair and place both your feet flat on the floor. Do not slouch. Rest your hands comfortably in your lap. Take a deep breath through your nose while extending your stomach. Push your stomach out as the air comes into and fills your lungs. Your shoulders can rise and possibly go back a bit.

Place one hand on your chest and the other on your abdomen. Which hand rises most? If it is the hand on your abdomen, then you are breathing properly. If not, pull your breath deeper into your lungs. Once your lungs are full, hold the air to the count of six and then let the air escape naturally out of your nose, as if you were letting it slowly out of a balloon.

As you exhale, your shoulders will fall and your extended stomach will come back in, helping to complete the deep exhalation of used air. Repeat, taking each deep breath slowly through the nose. Do this warm-up 10 times, and concentrate on the sound of the air going in and out of your nose.

## THE FAST-TRACK ROUTINE

While the basic routine is a good warm-up to use when you have spare time before a practice or before the event at which you are giving your presentation, you may need a quick refresher as you sit at your table waiting to be introduced. At the same time, your fast-track routine will give you that slight calm needed to get the butterflies in your stomach flying in formation.

### *Body Refresher 1: Deep Breath/Body Tense*

As you sit, take a deep breath in through your nose and tighten everything in your body, from your head, neck, shoulders, hands, and fingers, down to your legs and toes. Hold the breath for six seconds, and then slowly let go of the tension in your body as you exhale through your mouth.

### *Body Refresher 2: Deep Breath/Clasp Hands*

As you sit, take a deep breath and clasp your hands together. Hold your breath as you squeeze the palms of your hands together tightly enough to feel it in your diaphragm. Let go of your hands and breath at the same time.

What you are doing with these two body refreshers is slowing your heartbeat. It's the heartbeat that is pumping adrenalin through your body, making you excited and energetic. As you slow down your heartbeat, you reduce the surge of adrenalin. Tensing, relaxing, and holding your breath will also empty your mind of any last-minute reservations you may have about giving your speech. You will feel more in control and calmer without diminishing the edge you need to be effective.

## A NOTE FOR SKEPTICS

The preceding exercises work, and work well. If you feel foolish doing these warm-ups, remember that many Eastern cultures do exercises as part of their normal workday. I recently led a seminar for a huge Japanese-owned company in the United States that involves all employees in morning exercises; the PA system fills every workstation with 10 minutes of guided destressing stretches. No one has been laughing at this organization recently.

Each of the six warm-up exercises can also serve a secondary purpose. The afternoon can be a deadly time to speak to an audience, especially if they have eaten a large lunch. If you notice that people are sleepy, it may not indicate a lack of interest in your subject. They may be tired of sitting! Ask the audience to stand and do one or more of the body warm-ups as a one-minute stretch break.

Try to anticipate their needs by putting yourself in their place; imagine you have been sitting for as long as they have. After all, you are standing and moving around, and your adrenalin is flowing. Your audience does not have the same adrenalin benefits.

## INDULGE YOURSELF BEFORE BIG SPEECHES

When you indulge yourself you affirm your value and build yourself up for your big event. You are celebrating in advance; just as Olympic athletes envision themselves celebrating a win. You create the mood of a winner.

My personal favorite indulgence before a speech that I know will require lots of energy is to relax myself with a shiatsu massage. I find my thinking becomes focused and my energy balanced after an hour of healing body work.

## INVESTIGATING THE AUDIENCE

You can combine some exercise before your presentation with some useful research by taking a short walk near the room where you will be speaking. This will help get rid of some of the adrenalin coursing through your veins while allowing you to shake hands with and talk to some of the people in your audience.

Since speaking is audience-centered, the more you know about your audience (see Chapter 8), the better your presentation will be. This is also a good way to calm down. As you introduce yourself and talk with people, you will find it difficult to concentrate on your fear about speaking.

Whether you use the basic routine, the fast-track routine, or walk before your presentation, recognize that speaking is a physically demanding as well as an intellectually challenging activity. Preparing your body by warming it up and channeling some of the nervous excitement will help you give your best presentation.

# 3

## NONVERBAL COMMUNICATION

*What you do speaks so*
*loudly I can not hear what*
*you're saying.*
    *—George Bernard Shaw*

How you say something is more important than what you say. The "how" encompasses nonverbal signals such as what you wear, how you stand, and your facial expressions and gestures. Other visual signals include your eye contact, gestures, movements, or other aspects of yourself seen by the audience.

Nonverbal signals may also be vocal: the pitch, volume, and speed of your voice; or how you use pauses for effect. These vocal signals are received along with your verbal message.

Your challenge in improving your presentation skills is to make these signals support your message as much as possible. For example, imagine that you are a surgeon coming from the operating room to speak to the family of your patient. You want them to understand the seriousness of the situation, and to understand that you care about them.

- Which entrance will you make?
- Do you enter the waiting room and sit down, or stand?

- Do you place your hand on the shoulder of a family member, or fold your arms in front of you?

- Do you make eye contact and speak slowly, or do you rush through the details and glance at the clock on the wall?

Each choice that you make affects how your message is received and understood.

## THE IMPORTANCE OF NONVERBAL COMMUNICATION

Before the 1960s, the teaching of speech and debate concerned only verbal skills. On September 26, 1960, a dramatic event—the first televised Kennedy-Nixon debate—changed the study of speech. Those who listened to the debate on radio thought that Richard Nixon had won.

The estimated 80 million people who watched the debate on television thought that the suntanned and fit-looking John Kennedy had prevailed over a white and pasty-faced Richard Nixon. The candidates' nonverbal signals turned the tables for the viewing audience.

Rock videos represent another example of how nonverbal signals affect a verbal message. Listen to a rock tune on your car radio for its musical merits alone. Watch the same rock tune as a music video and see if you are distracted from the quality of the music by jerky film edits or are intrigued by the use of erotic messages to sell the song.

A study from the University of California at Los Angeles (UCLA) indicates that, as startling as it seems, more than 90 percent of what an audience believes and trusts comes from visual and vocal signals. The verbal message—the content of the words— accounts for only 7 percent of the impact on an audience. *If you are visually congruent and vocally enthusiastic, you increase an audience's attention to your verbal message and enhance your credibility.*

Nonverbal signals are important for two reasons. First, you can use them to become a better speaker. If your nonverbal signals are distracting, your audience won't focus on your verbal message. Second, as a listener, you can more readily cut through nonverbal signals and concentrate on the verbal messages you receive from others, hence reducing the degree to which you're affected by image.

Many poor speakers have useful information that may be overlooked because of inappropriate visual and vocal signals.

## VISUAL SIGNALS

You can recognize visual signals and delivery techniques that impact your message and make them support, rather than detract, from what you have to say:

### Clothing

If you know your audience and the purpose of your presentation, you can choose clothes that will enhance your presentation in a management setting.  For men, a suit obviously demonstrates more authority than a sportscoat or blazer.

However, if your meeting is in Hawaii or Florida and many members of your audience are in short-sleeve shirts or sportscoats, then a suit may not be a wise choice. It's best to ask the person who has scheduled you to speak what the audience will likely be wearing and what would be most appropriate for you.

For men, dark cool-toned colors, such as navy blue, gray, and black, communicate power and authority on a subconscious level. Big men, though, will want to stay away from black because it can be intimidating. Keeping the suit jacket closed gives the impression of a broad chest and narrow waist. White shirts are always appropriate, along with silk ties, high-rise socks, and polished leather shoes.

Women have more flexibility with color and style. They do not have to dress like men to give a successful speech. Dress needs to be planned from awareness of your message. Avoid skirts that are too short and too tight. Also check to see that there are no runs in your stockings (always carry an extra pair) and that your shoes are comfortable and conservative. It would be a shame to lose credibility because you were unaware of the impact of your clothing's message. I watched a well trained, highly skilled administrative assistant present an overview of a complicated computer system to a group of senior managers. Verbally she was fantastic. If we had played a tape recording of her presentation, the men in her audience would have heard her. Unfortunately, because of her short skirt, dangly earrings, and low-cut blouse she was not taken seriously. If you are giving a speech, you want to deliver a message of quality information, not sexuality. Dress for business when you are in a business environment—dress for play when you plan to play.

Color is important. Find out which colors look best on you and wear them. In fact, you can go one step better and organize your wardrobe around them. A professional image consultant, Lydia Young, helped me to design a wardrobe that would meet my needs. She taught me the importance of color, suit style, and wardrobe planning. If you recognize you need help in this area, ask a professional image consultant to give you a core wardrobe session.

Purchase either loosely fitted jackets or quality suits that are tailored to fit you. When trying on clothes before buying them, run through several gestures to further determine what constitutes a good fit. A poorly fitting suit is a distraction, particularly if you are overweight.

Imagine trying to give a presentation wearing new shoes that are rubbing painful blisters on your feet. Break in shoes long before speech time; in front of an audience is not the place to experiment with new shoes or clothes.

If you wear contacts or glasses, avoid tinted lenses. People want to see your eyes when you speak. Fortunately, nonglare, nontint lenses are available today. (No granny glasses please; they are distracting and will age you.) Also, do not wear jewelry that is large, distracting, or noisy.

*Why Bother with These Tips?*   You exude more confidence when you've paid attention to details. It's as if you were putting on the lab coat of a doctor, the black robe of a judge, or the uniform of a police officer. You look neat, you feel you have taken on the trappings of expertise, and people perceive you within the context of your image. Like an actor, you can become the person you are dressed to be.

If you follow these suggestions daily, all the better. You never know when you might be called into an important meeting. Dress as if something is going to happen.

## Posture and Movement

Posture is a highly visual element of your speech. Does your current posture distract from your message? Often, unpracticed speakers will sway or rock at the podium. Try this: Stand up and spread your feet a comfortable distance apart, four to eight inches, parallel to each other, and pointed straight ahead. Flex your knees and put your weight on the balls of your feet. The space and symmetry of this position will stop any swaying or rocking motion, and will diminish any distracting heel movements.

Moving is important when you speak. When done naturally, it relaxes both the audience and you. When you move, take at least two steps and get back into position. Avoid pacing; it is extremely distracting—unless you are Tom Peters and it's your personal trademark! Use your movement to establish contact with people in all parts of the room. Depending on the purpose of your presentation and on your audience, you may even want to walk to the back of the room occasionally.

Getting close to your listeners by varying the distance between yourself and the audience increases both their attention and interest. After all, they won't know when you may be walking up to them. Closing the distance also will encourage people to respond if you are asking questions.

A distance of 12 to 25 feet or more is considered a public distance zone. In training situations, you can approach each attendee within a social distance of 4 to 12 feet often, and within a personal distance of 18 inches to 4 feet now and then.

Face the audience head-on and hold your shoulders squarely. Tilting to the side is usually interpreted as being less open or interested. Keep your posture open. Crossing your arms in front of you may be perceived as a sign of defensiveness. Keep your arms relaxed and hanging down at your side when you are not using them to gesture. In fact, keeping your entire body relaxed and loose conveys openness and helps combat nervousness.

*Reverse the Process.*   As you may have guessed, you can use many of the techniques discussed in this chapter to get feedback on audience response. If you notice clusters of nonverbals such as people crossing their arms on their chests, leaning back, and avoiding your eye contact, switch gears in your presentation to reawaken interest:

- Verbally, you can condense part of your presentation.
- Vocally, you can change your pitch or tone of voice.
- Visually, you can move to and address a different part of the room or gesture more vividly to regain attention.

Another crucial aspect of posture is to hold your head in a comfortable position with the chin up. The position of your chin matters: The chin down is the typical pattern of acquiescence. As speaker, you are the expert, you are in charge. Any nonverbal signals that contradict your authority will detract from your presentation.

If you practice your posture each day as you speak to others one-on-one, it will become comfortable and natural to you.


## Eye Communication

Making eye contact with people in your audience can be difficult. You might fear seeing disapproval or boredom, or losing your train of thought. Yet, if you don't achieve eye contact, you aren't relating to anyone, and if you're not relating to your audience, you are not going to get your message across.

Catching one friendly face and delivering your presentation to that person is ineffective. Staring is combative, and some people simply do not like to be looked at. If you make eye contact with someone who quickly turns away, try not to look directly into that person's eyes again. Some cultures do not feel it is appropriate to look directly into other people's eyes.

When you look at an audience, a "Z" formation will help you gain more effective eye contact. Start with a familiar or friendly face. Look at that person for 3 to 5 seconds, long enough to finish a thought or idea, and then move on, in a "Z" around the room. Rather than starting at one end of the Z and proceeding repeatedly to the other, break your Z by starting from the middle sometimes, or the back, to vary your eye contact.

Another effective technique is the "nod." Periodically nod to someone and you'll notice that he or she nods back. Too much nodding, however, can have a yo-yo effect.

I knew a woman who had left her job on maternity leave. Upon returning, she was speaking to a group of people, when suddenly she found herself nodding almost constantly. She realized that during her three months at home with a baby, she had grown so accustomed to exaggerating her head movements as she talked to her newborn that she was now doing it with adults!

## Facial Expressions

We all need to be aware of our smile. Some of us may overuse the smile in an effort to appear gracious, or because we are nervous. It is difficult to speak when you're smiling all the time.

A simple rule for most women is to smile when you feel like smiling—when the feeling is genuine.

Men typically need to smile more. Some put a damper on company meetings through dour expression, even when the news is good. To up your smile quotient, either videotape yourself giving a presentation or enlist a friend to help. Note the number of times you smile during a talk. If you look too serious, repeat your speech a few times with the goal of smiling more. Draw a few happy faces at various places in your outline to remind yourself to smile.

## VOCAL SIGNALS

### Pitch

Variety in your voice puts spice and interest in your presentation. Pitch is how high or low your voice registers. We all have a range to work with and can only take it down so low. Stress or nervousness makes voices get higher. Research shows that the deeper the pitch of your voice, the longer people will listen to you. George Bush has a high-pitched voice, as opposed to a low-pitched Robert Dole.

---

**CONTROLLING YOUR PITCH**

This activity will demonstrate the flexibility of your own voice, and show you how to use the lower range of your pitch. Repeat the following three sentences—each time at a deeper pitch:

1. "This is my normal pitch."
2. "Do, Re, Me, Fa, So, La, Te, Do"
3. "This is my normal voice."

Now stop.

Did you hear a difference between the first sentence and the last? Repeat the trio of sentences until you are in control of your pitch and can deepen it at will.

If you practice this exercise 10 times each day, after six weeks you will have greater control over your pitch.

---

## *Volume*

Volume is the loudness or softness of your voice. You want to control and offer variety in volume as you speak. If you speak softly the whole time, you won't hold people's attention. Elizabeth Taylor is a soft-spoken individual, particularly when she is speaking about AIDS research or selling her perfume, *Passion*. She is so strikingly beautiful, however, that her appearance alone commands attention and compensates for her lack of volume. Not many of us can make that claim.

People who yell often, such as Morton Downey, Jr. (he goaded everyone on his short-lived talk show to yell as well) are particularly difficult to listen to. Variety and audibility are the keys.

Two exercises can help you have greater control over your volume:

1. Breathe from your diaphragm and speak as if your voice is hitting the back wall, or 10 rows behind the last person in your audience. If you breathe from your diaphragm, you'll have more air flow and also avoid sore throats.
2. Have a friend record the first few minutes of a speech with a tape recorder, while carrying it from the front to the back row. At first it may seem as if you are screaming, but listen to the tape and see how you sound. Keep practicing until the tape recorder picks up your voice from the back row and you feel comfortable projecting as you speak.

## *Rate*

Rate is how fast you are speaking. Normal speaking is 120 to 150 words per minute. Listen to yourself and others in a normal one-on-one conversation. If people consistently cut you off, you are probably going too slow. If people ask, "What did you say?" slow down, you are probably going too fast.

Try this exercise: Clip 150 words from a magazine or newspaper article and read it using a stop watch or the second hand on a clock to measure how fast you talk. Based on your results, slow down or speed up your speech. You will be able to see improvement in just three minutes of practice each day.

Reading books to your children is excellent practice, and it benefits them, too. Be dramatic, time yourself, and experiment with the pitch, volume, and rate of your voice. Also pay attention to the two vocal "Ps": punch and pause.

## Punch

In every sentence, one word or phrase is more important than the rest. Read this sentence out loud: "The company was forced to ask him for his resignation." If you were a company spokesperson, you might consider "forced" to be the most important word. If you were a colleague of the person told to resign, you might consider "resignation" to be the key word.

Whatever your choice, you want to emphasize that word or phrase to make your point to your audience. This technique is called "punching" it. Speech writers underline the words they want the speaker to hit. You can do the same on your outline.

## Pause

In written language, punctuation identifies pauses. In spoken language, we also have pauses. Some pauses come when we are nervous, such as "um," "hm," and "you know." Those nervous pauses need to be eliminated.

Other pauses, the kind that frame an idea, can be very effective. In 1968, Lyndon Johnson announced on television that he would not run for a second term as President. His statement was rewritten several times by himself, his wife, and several speech writers. With a dramatic pause following each comma, he gave the nation the final version: "Accordingly, I shall not seek, and I will not accept, the nomination of my party for another term as your President."

John Wayne was a master of the pause. Watch any of his movies, and you will see how "Duke" stole scene after scene from his fellow actors, simply by pausing at the most dramatic moment.

### Sentence Closure

Have you ever listened to a speaker who finished sentences with rising intonation? It sounds as if the person is asking a question rather speaking with authority. Similarly, swallowing, or tailing off, the last few words of a sentence reduces a speaker's impact.

Finish each sentence completely and with clarity, keeping your volume up while dropping your pitch. Walter Cronkite, longtime anchor for CBS News, had a familiar farewell at the end of his newscasts that represents a good example of sentence closure (though it may have held little truth for the people whose issues weren't covered in the newscast):

". . . and that's the way it is, Wednesday, April 14, 1965."

## BEFORE YOU START TO SPEAK, "SOFTEN"

SOFTEN is an acronym for much of what was covered in this chapter:

| S | = | Smile | Smile in a genuine way. |
|---|---|---|---|
| O | = | Open stance | Keep body and arms open to the audience. |
| F | = | Forward lean | Put weight on balls of your feet. |
| T | = | Tone | Check the pitch, volume, rate of your voice. |
| E | = | Eye contact | Make a "Z" of eye communication in the room. |
| N | = | Nod | Nod from time to time. |

Keep this acronym in mind when you stand up to begin your speech, and you'll be off to a good start.

# 4

# *USING GESTURES EFFECTIVELY*

*A gesture is a movement
which you make and hold
for at least five seconds.
Anything else is merely a
nervous mannerism.*
   *—Patricia Fripp*

Gestures are nonverbal signals that serve as visual reinforcements for a key word or idea that you're communicating to your audience. Gestures include hand and arm movements.

When speaking one-on-one, we often don't think about our hands. Somehow, when before an audience, we become terrified. Suddenly our hands feel as awkward and obvious as brightly colored balloons inflating on the ends of our arms. In our efforts to deflate or disguise the balloons, we try many things. Unfortunately, most of our Band-Aid solutions are ineffective.

## NEGATIVE GESTURES

Men who are nervous tend to adopt the "at ease" stance of a sailor standing on the deck of an aircraft carrier. They cross their hands behind their backs, and we never see those appendages again. Or,

**FIGURE 4.1**

they cross their hands low in front, like a fig leaf of protection against the immodesty of speaking to an audience (see Figure 4.1).

Both men and women sometimes cross their arms over their chests in an effort to look confident and relaxed, but the body language often translates into defensiveness to onlookers. With crossed arms, not only are you closed to the audience, you will feel as if you are holding yourself in (see Figure 4.2).

As a test, fold your arms over your chest now. If you're like most people, it will make you feel uncommunicative. Since the purpose of your presentation is to communicate with the audience, you'll want to avoid making any gestures that could inhibit the information exchange.

As shown in Figure 4.3, putting your hands in your pockets is risky because of the temptation to play with your change or keys; the constant jangle is distracting. Some people have trouble getting their hands back out again and pull

**FIGURE 4.2**   Crossed arms: Hands crossed in front can exhibit the feeling of openness and hence the information exchange.

**FIGURE 4.3** Hands in pockets: With the hands in pockets, the temptation to play with loose change is too great. It also inhibits communication through hand gestures.

their pockets inside out in the process. Men should take the change out of their pockets before any presentation to avoid the temptation of playing with the coins when under stress.

When attempting to control your hands, there is also the danger of locking them down, such as folding them in a prayer stance on the podium. This gesture pulls in your energy, rather than letting it reach out to the audience.

In a effort to use gestures, many of us perform weak hand twirls and wiggles on top of the podium, or even behind it; such movements are more appropriate for calling a dog's attention to under-the-table tidbits of food than for clarifying a point. Then, too, if your gestures are too low to be seen, they are useless (see Figure 4.4). Upward, open gestures are by far the most effective.

**FIGURE 4.4** Gestures to avoid: Gestures too low to be seen are useless.

# USING GESTURES APPROPRIATELY

### Gestures Are Relaxing

Among the many benefits of using appropriate gestures is that they help you relax as a speaker. Just as athletes use stretching exercises to warm up before a competition, you can use gestures to relax yourself as you speak and to minimize stage fright.

Gestures also help relax your audience. Listeners feel more at ease with a speaker who gestures comfortably.

- Cheerleaders use gestures at basketball and football games to lead fans in cheers that both relieve the tension of a close game and bond the group to support the team.

- Before taping game or talk shows, television studios have someone warm up the audience with a few jokes, to get them used to the idea that it is desirable to react to what they see by applauding, laughing, or cheering.
  On a lesser scale, you are doing the same thing for your audience as you speak and gesture—you are warming them up, and guiding them to react to your ideas. Relaxing your audience initiates a mutually beneficial cycle. Since they are relaxed, you will be more relaxed as you speak.

### Gestures Emphasize Your Ideas

Gestures help you emphasize the important points in your speech. When do you use them? You may gesture to reinforce a word or to draw people toward an idea that you are expressing. Gesturing backs up a verbal message with a visual one. In addition, the physical act of gesturing increases your energy, hence you'll work toward the key point of your speech with greater vitality.

Gestures work best when they are uninhibited and spontaneous. They come from what you feel, or from the idea you are trying to express. Don't practice canned gestures ahead of time; you'll look phony.

We've all seen the television commercials featuring testimonials by chief executive officers or business owners. They *try* to look casual sitting at a desk or reaching for a book while reciting a 30-second sales pitch, but it's obviously staged and phony. They are not trained as actors to look spontaneous.

While spontaneity is not something you can practice, there are some specific suggestions that you can follow in making gestures to emphasize your ideas.

## SUGGESTIONS FOR USING GESTURES

Gestures are best employed when they support your delivery, not when they overwhelm it. If you use gestures sparingly, only when needed to emphasize the major points of your speech, they will be more effective.

When you gesture, use the upper quadrant of your body, and make your gestures up and out to the audience. You want your movements to be broad and flowing, not quick and jerky. The best gestures are a natural extension of yourself. Take the time to make them smooth as you express your thoughts (see Figure 4.5).

Vary your gestures, and avoid those that seem trite, stale, or commonplace. It's easy to fall into the habit of making the same motion repeatedly. While the repetition might be helpful to your thought process, it can be as distracting to your audience as playing with your watch or twirling a strand of your hair while you speak.

Some gestures interfere with the ability of your audience to listen to you. For instance, don't use your fist to gesture or point your finger at your audience. People find that threatening—think about the last time someone pointed at you!

Instead, use your palms and open them out to your audience. Send your gestures up and out where they will be visible. Move the arm and hand as a single unit; this will eliminate any suggestion of weak, floppy wrists or elbows.

**FIGURE 4.5**  Practicing winning gestures: (a) Palms opened are a positive gesture; (b) gesturing with one or two arms can emphasize what you are saying; (c) sweeping motions of an arm can enhance communication; keep the gestures varied so as not to become stale.

Relate the extent of your gestures to the size of your audience and your distance from them. Large audiences need bigger gestures. If you are speaking in a medium-size or small room, reduce your gestures a little.

The best way to assess your gestures is to stand in front of a mirror and practice. You will soon realize that what feels awkward may look fantastic and what feels comfortable sends out the wrong message.

Last but not least, a simple nod of the head can emphasize a point, and a smile suggests confidence. As a speaker who uses gestures effectively, you will be projecting your ease, confidence, and authority.

# 5

# *STAYING IN CONTROL*

**Self-conquest is the
greatest of all victories.**
**—Plato**

In the Olympic games, athletes bring their coaches with them;
not surprisingly, many of these coaches are trained in psychology. It is their job to keep the athletes thinking "win" not "fail."
When you get up to give a speech, do you think "win"? Negative
thinking is a self-fulfilling prophecy that can become a habit if
you use your mind in that way. Your subconscious mind believes
whatever you tell it.

Let the power of your subconscious help you. Picture yourself
in front of the audience. Your voice is firm and varies enough in
pitch and level to be interesting, the content flows in a logical
progression, and people in the audience are sitting forward in
their seats, intent on you. You've prepared, you've practiced,
you've emphasized your strengths and minimized your weaknesses. Think of yourself as a star, and remember the information
you're going to present is the audience's payoff.

Just before you get up to speak, possibly as you are being introduced, veteran speaking coach Dorothy Sarnoff recommends your
saying the following three things to yourself:

1. I'm glad I'm here!
2. I'm glad you're here!
3. I know I know!

Regardless of how well you mentally prep yourself to make a presentation, if you're not a little nervous, then you're not alive. Nervousness before speaking may cause you to overlook things such as a collar that is sticking straight up or a zipper that is still open. Physically, you may suffer from a mouth as dry as the Gobi Desert or perspiration that soaks an entire handkerchief.

In this chapter, we'll cover some basic tips for dealing with these concerns. The important point is to know yourself, know what eccentricities might apply to you, and be prepared so that the audience gets the best from you.

## WHAT TO DRINK AND WHEN

Before or during your speech, your mouth and throat may get dry because you are nervous or because talking brings in air that dries your mucous passages.

### Refresh Yourself

The best beverage to drink is *room-temperature water with a lemon*, even if you have to bring it yourself in a thermos in your briefcase. A dash of lemon helps because it diminishes any mucous buildup. Here's what to avoid drinking:

- *Do Not Drink Ice Water.* The ice will constrict your throat, and your voice will not be as rich.

- *Do Not Drink Milk or Eat Any Milk Products.* When you digest milk (or milk products, such as ice cream or yogurt), it curdles in the mouth and makes your dry mouth even worse. Also milk products coat your vocal cords and cause phlegm.

- *Do Not Drink Soda.* The carbonation can make you belch, the sugar can dry your throat, and the caffeine can make you jumpy.

- *Do Not Drink Coffee or Tea.* Again, the caffeine content can have a negative effect.

- *Absolutely Do Not Drink Alcohol.* Even if you have just eaten dinner and are about to give the after-dinner speech, the stress involved in giving a presentation will make your blood rush to your brain. If you drink alcohol, it will rush to your brain along with the blood and will relax you. But you don't want to be too relaxed, *you want to be sharp!*

### Bite Your Tongue

If no room-temperature water is available, you can always rely on the last-resort technique of biting your tongue. This will cause your glands to produce saliva, which in turn will moisten your mouth.

### Use Vaseline

If you have to do a lot of smiling and talking, such as in a receiving line at an important business dinner, a dab of Vaseline can help. Put a little on your finger and rub it over the front of your teeth to create a thin film of moisture that will keep your upper lip from sticking to your teeth if your mouth is dry. Beauty contestants use this technique to keep their smiles smooth and fluid.

## AN ABSORBING PROBLEM

Perspiration is a common problem encountered by speakers. We are all prone to sweat when feeling nervous, confronting hot lights, or speaking in a closed room. A simple solution is to apply unscented talcum powder to your body ahead of time. Skiers put it in their socks to absorb perspiration and to keep their feet from getting cold.

Sprinkle a light coating of talcum powder on your body. It will protect you for most of the morning. If you are scheduled to speak in the afternoon or evening, pack a small container of powder in your briefcase or purse. When you apply the powder, remember to put it on your hands away from any dark-colored clothing you might be wearing. Then double-check for any "snow" in the mirror before you leave. Women will find it effective to purchase a translucent or colorless powder that applies lightly over their makeup yet does not coat the face noticeably.

If you are prone to sweat profusely, carry a cotton handkerchief. When you need to use it, do so, and then put it away. Even if you use the handkerchief several times during a speech, it won't be distracting if you remember to use and put it away immediately. It's more distracting to watch someone perspire.

## COOL IT DOWN

Before you start your presentation, check the room thermostat with the sponsor or whoever is in charge of arrangements. A hot and stuffy room will drain you and your audience of energy. Besides adding to any perspiration problem you may have, people are more likely to fall asleep in a warm room.

Whenever possible, I set the room temperature at 68 degrees Fahrenheit. This is just cool enough to keep the audience from getting heavy-eyelid syndrome, but not to make them shiver. If the weather is cooperative and you are in a room with windows that open, use the windows to ensure a good air flow.

## MIRROR, MIRROR ON THE WALL

Some people prepare for speaking in almost every possible way; they know the content of the information they want to present, have practiced delivery of the speech, and understand the audience to which they are presenting the information. Yet, they do not take the time to check their appearance before going "on."

Imagine all the things you fix during a last-minute check before you leave your home in the morning and how embarrassed you are if you have missed something important. When you're standing in front of an audience, your embarrassment doubles and adds to your anxiety about what else might be wrong.

Before you leave to give your presentation, check the mirror (a full-length mirror is best). A quick look can catch the hanging slip, the lipstick on the teeth, the stray cowlick of hair, or the unzipped fly! The seconds needed for the examination are worth it.

## LAUGHING AWAY THE SPLOTCHES

When fair or thin-skinned people are nervous, they often become red and splotchy, especially around the neck and cheeks, because blood is rushing through the body. Women may help disguise the effect by wearing suits, scarves, or high-collared blouses in varying shades of red or pink, or using a rouge to offset the color in their faces.

The best cure for nervousness is to relax, and one of the best ways to do so is to use humor. That's why many people begin their speeches with a humorous anecdote or "ice breaker." Laughing causes the brain to release a chemical called an endorphin, which is a tranquilizer or relaxer. Humor can make both you and your audience feel good.

To use humor effectively, however, you have to feel comfortable. Practice to perfect your timing so that you can sound as if you are speaking off the cuff. How do you judge what is humorous and worth using? Here are four criteria:

1. *You Have to Remember the Punch Line.* Many a speaker has been eager to relate a great story only to forget the punch line. Few stories can stand on their own. If you forget the punch line, the audience is likely to either doubt your credibility or feel sorry for you (or both). Neither response is desirable.

2. *The Story Relates to the Subject of Your Speech.* If your audience is composed of spouses of disabled people and you are speaking about how to build a network of support, an anecdote about football probably is inappropriate.

3. *Your Timing Is Good.* Practice your anecdote. Tell it to several different people and watch their reactions. Practice until you feel comfortable.

4. *Most Importantly, Tell a Story That Is at No One's Expense.* You might think a joke about an overweight woman is OK because your audience is all male, and you don't see any obese persons in the room. Wrong! You don't know who the members of your audience live with or what their values are; *any time you put down or offend someone in any way, even in a humorous way, it is not funny.*

The best humor comes from your personal experiences, when you can laugh at yourself and share it with others. Although you don't want to depreciate yourself, you do want show that you are human.

To gather humorous anecdotes from your daily life, you need to write them in a notebook as soon as they happen. Many parents of young children make a mental note of the funny things their children do in the course of a day. But rarely do they actually remember these experiences later, or write them down for their children's baby books.

Get a small pocket notebook and carry it with you. When something humorous happens, write it down. In a year, you'll probably have an entire collection of anecdotes to enhance a presentation.

## SUMMARY: STAYING IN CHARGE

Use the following checklist on the morning of your presentation to ensure you haven't forgotten any last-minute details.

It doesn't matter how good your verbal presentation is if people are staring at a popping button, an unzipped fly, or a skirt that is too short. They will be so busy paying attention to those distracting details that your message may become lost. Your visual message must complement your verbal message for people to hear you.

## CHECKLIST: STAYING IN CHARGE

| *Problem* | *Solutions* |
|---|---|
| Dry mouth | Plain water*<br>Biting your tongue<br>Petroleum jelly* |
| Sweating | Translucent powder*<br>Makeup powder*<br>Handkerchief*<br>Check of room temperature |
| Embarrassing appearance | Checking in front of full-length mirror<br>Asking an associate |
| Red splotches | Pink or red-toned clothing<br>Accent scarves*<br>Rouge*<br>Relaxing with humor |

* You may need to bring these items from home.

# GROUNDWORK

## *WHAT'S IN IT FOR YOU*

Chapter 6 discusses various styles of delivering a presentation. Frequently the situation dictates the style you use. Speakers need to be aware of the options, and the benefits and disadvantages of each.

Chapter 7 will give you the 10 steps to prepare a presentation. Step by step, you will build your next presentation starting with selecting your topic based on your purpose, audience, and the details of your speaking situation. The chapter ends with ideas for putting together your final draft. This chapter previews the upcoming information.

Status, size, demographics, and attitudes influence what and how you will present. In Chapter 8, you will learn how each of these factors affects your preparation. A sample Feedback Sheet will help you gain valuable feedback so that each time you present you are able to improve.

In Chapter 9, you'll be able to analyze your audience by answering the questions provided. Once you've done your analysis, you will know how to tailor your presentation to your specific audience.

# 6

## STYLES OF DELIVERY

*"It takes about 3 weeks to prepare a good impromptu speech."*
—*Mark Twain*

There are five basic types of speech or presentation delivery. The following chart identifies them and their appropriate uses in different speaking situations. We will then explore each of these styles.

### IMPROMPTU STYLE

Impromptu speeches are given on the spur of the moment, or "off the cuff." You are not informed in advance that you will be called on, and you get up to speak.

Most presentations are impromptu. In a common scenario, you are at a business meeting and are asked to speak on a project. You haven't had time to prepare, and as you scramble for facts in your mind, you might also see your life flashing before your eyes. However, after the initial panic, you may be surprised how well you do, if you relax and let the facts surface.

## FIVE STYLES OF DELIVERY

| Delivery Style | Description | When to Use |
|---|---|---|
| Impromptu | Off the cuff | Speaking without warning or time to prepare |
| | | Often used in meetings |
| Extemporaneous | Planned Prepared Practiced Spoken from an outline | Most planned speaking |
| Expromptu | Prepared but not practiced | Most business meetings |
| | | Last-minute substitute speaker |
| Manuscript | Written and read word for word | Scientific conferences |
| | | Political gatherings |
| | | When someone else writes the speech |
| Memorized | Recited word for word from a manuscript. | Don't use it! |

Impromptu speeches can be a disaster if you don't know what you are talking about. Many businesspeople can use impromptu speaking as a tool for testing their knowledge, and the knowledge of their colleagues. In a roundtable setting, impromptu speaking can become brainstorming sessions, resulting in some new ideas for business application.

In a similar way, actors use a kind of impromptu speaking called improvisation to test their acting skills and extract knowledge from the depths of their minds. Success in impromptu speaking comes with being able to relax and free your mind to pour out the facts that you know.

## EXTEMPORANEOUS STYLE

Extemporaneous speeches are given after you have the opportunity to prepare for the delivery. Extemporaneous speaking is planned, prepared, and practiced. You may use an outline or notes, but never write the speech out or memorize it. Every time you deliver it, the information needs to be a little different.

This is the delivery most frequently used by speakers. On Nelson Mandela's tour of the United States and 14 other countries in 1990, he spoke extemporaneously on the same subject in every major city that he visited. Each time, however, his message sounded slightly different.

His intentions were to speak about the goals of his political group and to raise money. In each American city, he was able to adapt this message to his particular audience, and to the region of the country in which he was speaking.

An extemporaneous speech may sound spontaneous, but each detail is thought out in advance. This style of delivery gives you the flexibility to move ideas around and change things to adapt to the specific needs of your particular audience.

## EXPROMPTU STYLE

Expromptu speeches are a hybrid, a combination of extemporaneous and impromptu styles of delivery. You have time to prepare, but not to practice. This kind of delivery occurs when a meeting is called and you have no time to practice or when you participate in a debate, where you are allowed note cards or conference time with teammates and a short period to collect your thoughts, but you speak with no practice.

The success of expromptu speaking depends on your outline or the collection of your thoughts. Any time you have notice of a presentation, however, take the time to practice.

## MANUSCRIPT STYLE

Speeches given from a manuscript are exactly that. The speech is written down, word for word, and you deliver it by reading your manuscript, word for word, to the audience.

This style of delivery is the mainstay of scientific conferences, where written papers are submitted months in advance, a few are chosen because of their technical quality, and the authors then read them to the body of the conference, as written.

Politicians also use manuscript speeches, written usually by a staff speech writer. Teachers and trainers sometimes use manuscript speeches when exact wording is required. Because teachers and trainers try to fit a lot of information into a structured time period, such as a week-long or semester-long course, word choice can be crucial and timing needs to be exact. The manuscript style of delivery answers these needs.

Manuscript speeches are hard to deliver effectively, however. You start reading your paper and your audience goes to sleep. With the manuscript style of delivery, you must:

- Make copies of your speech.
- Pass them out to the audience.
- Talk about the *highlights* of your manuscript.

Otherwise, you'll surely lose the audience. Since in most cases you don't have this flexibility, it is best to stay away from manuscript delivery altogether.

If you need to write your material before giving it as a speech, write it as if you were talking. Oral and written language have obvious differences, and people are not accustomed to hearing the written word used in language.

Use short sentences and write in contractions. Use large type, underlines, and triple spacing. Indicate pauses and places where you want to make eye contact. Then, practice with the manuscript so that you can deliver the message comfortably.

If you must read from a manuscript, use the scope technique—slide your thumb and pointer finger down the page, scoping one section at a time. This helps you to find your place after you look up at your audience.

## *MEMORIZED STYLE*

Watch any awards show on television and you will see acceptance speeches that cover all five styles of delivery discussed here. The most painful speeches to watch, however, are those of people who struggle to recall memorized speeches when they face millions of people—excited that they have actually won the coveted award, their minds and faces go blank.

Memorized speeches are those that you write down on paper, memorize, and attempt to deliver word for word from memory. My advice is *NEVER* to use this style of delivery. First, you will stand before your audience with a blank look as you struggle to remember each word. Second, as discussed earlier, there is a difference between oral and written language.

Oral language consists of short sentences and phrases, contractions, slang, and starts and stops. Written language consists of longer, more formal sentences with transitions. It looks fluent on paper, but it doesn't flow when you speak.

You have little chance of being successful with memorized or manuscript speeches because they do not allow you to engage in heightened conversation. The content of conversation depends on how the other person responds to your statement, question, or discussion. As a speaker, you depend on cues from the audience to guide your delivery, adapting it, when necessary, to meet their needs. Obviously, that's not possible when you are reading or reciting a speech. Throughout the balance of this book, we will focus on expromptu and extemporaneous speaking.

# 7

# *STEPS IN PREPARING A PRESENTATION*

*For every disciplined effort
there is a multiple reward.*
*—Jim Rohn*

In this chapter, we will give you an overview of the steps for preparing your presentation. As with acquiring any new skill, the more you practice the better you'll be.

The following chapters provide more detail on several of these speech preparation steps. They are not complicated and don't take long to prepare. I do much of my speech preparation in my car, because I am often on the road.

If six hours are available to prepare a speech, many people will spend four of those hours complaining and procrastinating. Remember the power of your mind focused on a task will lead to greater creativity. Tell yourself this is something you want to do and remind yourself of the benefits to you. Get going!

---

### STEPS FOR PREPARING A SPEECH

1. Select or tailor a topic based on your purpose, your audience, and the details of your speaking situation.
2. Limit the topic to one central theme.
3. Collect data about the subject.
4. Select a method of organization.
5. Outline the main points; use three to five points to support your central theme.
6. Gather supporting information, such as stories to support your main points.
7. Check for accuracy.
8. Design a catchy, energetic introduction.
9. Write a strong conclusion.
10. Put together your final draft.

The 10 steps are supported by five additional steps:

11. Practice.
12. Practice.
13. Practice.
14. Practice.
15. Practice.

---

## SELECTING OR TAILORING A TOPIC

If you are speaking in connection with your work, your topic most likely has already been dictated by either your specific area of expertise, the occasion, or by your manager. Nevertheless, here are three things you will want to ask yourself:

- What is my *P*URPOSE for giving the speech?
- Who is in my *A*UDIENCE?
- What are the *L*OGISTICS?

Think of this as your PAL.

## What Is My Purpose for Giving the Speech?

If the purpose of your speech is to inform your audience, then you need to give them new and useful information. If the purpose of your speech is to persuade your audience, then you want to make them believe something or call them to some action.

What do you hope to accomplish by the end of your speech? You have to know the end result—new knowledge, a new belief, or a call to action—before you can develop the information for your presentation.

## Who Is in the Audience?

To relate your speech to the audience and understand how you can make an impact on them, you need to know who they are—a theme that cannot be overemphasized. You can't make speaking an audience-centered sport if you don't know who the players are!

Before you select a topic, gather all the demographic information about your audience, such as number of listeners, age, sex, race, religion, educational background, their attitude about you and the subject, and work-related experience. Learn their level of interest in your potential subject. Your goal is to tailor a subject that interests and accommodates as many of them as you can.

## Where Will I Speak and for How Long?

You need to know the details of the surroundings in which you will give your speech. For example, are you part of a team or panel of speakers? On what subjects will the others speak? Will you have a few minutes, an hour, or an afternoon to give your presentation?

Will you speak first thing in the morning, or after the lunch break? The answers to these questions are crucial factors in helping you tailor a topic. If you bypass these questions, and just jump into the preparation of your presentation, you will be missing vital information.

# LIMITING THE TOPIC

Winston Churchill was an outstanding orator who had his own formula for preparing a speech. His first step was to narrow the issue to one central theme—he limited his topic. Having determined your purpose for speaking, acquired a basic understanding of your audience, and learned the details of your presentation, you now limit your topic to a central theme.

Churchill believed that if you cannot state your theme in one sentence or less, then it is too broad. You may think that you need to give your audience everything you know or can gather on a particular subject, but people simply cannot absorb all that information. You are better off saying a lot about a little, than a little about a lot. Limit your topic according to the boundaries of the time you are allotted, particularly if you are trying to inform. Write your theme on paper and use it as a benchmark, holding you to your commitment to stay on track.

# COLLECTING DATA

Once you've limited your topic to a central theme, collect data. The first place to collect data is the subject matter expert: yourself. You may not have all the information you need, but you have enough to get started.

The best way to approach yourself for information is to brainstorm. Using a blank sheet of paper, write down key words and phrases about your subject. Putting what you know on paper helps you see where the holes in the information are, and what areas you need to research.

Sight-dominated people will appreciate having a blank wall where they can stick post-it notes with facts and stories for the speech. I use a large wall filled with different colored post-its to visualize my speech. I stand in front of the wall to do my first practice sessions. This always triggers creativity for me, and I can see how one section could be moved if needed. Using the post-its allows me to make changes to my outline with ease.

When I brainstorm about a topic, it generally takes no more than 10 minutes to outline the part I do know. Then I can clearly see what I need to investigate for more information.

Whenever you collect data, it has to be current and accurate, as well as relevant and acceptable to the people to whom you are speaking. For more detailed information on the type of data you may need and how to use it in your speech, see Chapter 13.

If you're already highly knowledgeable, then don't waste your time researching a familiar subject—it's an excuse not to get to work preparing your speech.

## SELECTING A METHOD OF ORGANIZATION

"Can you give me directions to the Museum of Modern Art?" If I stood in the lobby of a New York building and asked that question, I might get 20 different answers. I doubt that a single person would ask me if I intended to go by subway or by car—we are all very busy giving information from our point of view, but people receive it from their point of view. That's why the more you know about your audience, the easier it is to tailor your speech to meet their needs.

By selecting a method of organizing your speech, you are creating a road map of your subject, with your audience in mind, so that you can lead them from point A to point Z in a structured way. Don't jump around.

You can choose any of several ways to organize your speech, from telling events in time sequence, or chronological order, to presenting a proposition in your introduction and then proving it in the body of your speech. For more detailed information on speech organization, see Chapter 12.

When you are ready to select a method of organization, review the list of options and see what fits your subject best. For example, if your subject is "How to Use a Spread Sheet Program," you can see that there is spatial order: You are working with a confined space, and you are discussing using a personal computer in a new way. You still need to know your audience before starting your outline.

If I were giving this speech to adults attending community college who have no familiarity with spread sheets, I would start by talking about the ease of calculation once the rows and cells are set up. If I were talking to executives, I would begin by discussing how mastering spread sheets eliminates the need for layers of middle managers.

## OUTLINING THE MAIN POINTS

In his approach for preparing a speech, Churchill used one central theme and three main points. I expand on that and say it is acceptable to have up to five main points in the body of your speech. Because of our short-term-memory, we learn in chunks of information. If you attend a seminar on time management, and the instructor has one day to teach you everything you need to know, he or she will break the sessions down into chunks of information, so that while you will not remember everything, you will remember at least the main point in each of those segments. In a speech, unlike a book, your audience cannot quickly go back to a missed point.

For more detailed information on coming up with your key points, see Chapter 10.

## GATHERING SUPPORTING INFORMATION

After identifying three to five main points, you need to do your research. The information that will come from your research is likely to be dry facts and statistics. However, you want your audience to retain your key points. Enhance those points with secondary information that is as colorful as possible.

Tell stories, paint pictures, and use sounds and simple language so that your audience is listening to you and not scrambling to understand scientific words and jargon. Define words, compare and contrast ideas, quote the recognized experts in the field, and bring visual aids with you, such as graphic slides, so you can show as much as you tell.

This step will take the most time, but once you have gathered sufficient supporting information to enhance your main points, your speech preparation will be 80 percent complete. (See Chapter 13.)

## CHECKING FOR ACCURACY

Quickly review the six previous steps. Make sure that you have limited your topic and have developed your three to five main points satisfactorily. Verify that your information is accurate, current, and relevant.

## DESIGNING A CATCHY, ENERGETIC INTRODUCTION

A strong introduction is vital. It may seem as if we skipped a step—outlining your main points before writing your introduction—until you realize that you will not know how to introduce your main points unless you know what they are. As a guideline, the introduction needs to be 10 to 15 percent of your speech.

We all learned in basic high school composition classes:

- In the introduction, you tell them what you are going to tell them.
- In the body, you tell them.
- In the conclusion, you tell them what you told them.

In following that structure, plan the body of your speech first. The introduction is the most important part of the presentation. Grab your audience's interest from the beginning. If you don't get them to buy into your views early on, your chances of getting their attention later are minimal.

Your introduction serves four major purposes:

- It catches the attention of the audience and arouses interest.
- It previews the subject.
- It establishes WIIFT, or "what's in it for them."
- It establishes you as a credible source.

For more information on this step, see Chapter 11.

## WRITING A STRONG CONCLUSION

The conclusion comprises about 5 to 10 percent of your presentation and is easy to write because it is a reversal of the introduction. Again keep in mind, people learn through repetition and restatement. The conclusion has two parts: *a review of key points* (emphasize your three to five main points one more time), and *a memorable statement*.

The final statement of your presentation pulls your speech together. It could refer to the grabber statement in your introduction, be a challenge to the audience, or look to the future. End your presentation with strength, pride, and conviction.

If your subject has been a depressing one, you want your ending to be a call to action. It should give your audience a vision of what could be if they take action now. For more detailed information on this step, see Chapter 14.

## PUTTING TOGETHER YOUR FINAL DRAFT

Following the preceding steps will lead you to the final draft. Please copy your final draft. I know many cases where people have lost their speeches. Luggage gets lost, papers get thrown away accidentally, and briefcases get stolen. Leave one copy of your speech with someone at home, in case you need it faxed to you and your office is closed.

I recommend putting the speech in outline form on notepaper in a 14-point bold print with wide margins. Avoid using note cards. Because you can't get enough information on each card, you end up holding them and doing too much shuffling.

With paper, you can include far more information. Use only the top two thirds of the page, however. If you proceed all the way down the page, your eyes and your voice will drop and you will lose your audience's attention.

Your outline may consist of words in chronological order, where each word equates to a body of thought, or may consist of sentences that provide more information. Both of these forms of outlines have their drawbacks. With single words you may panic and forget what the word is supposed to prompt you to remember. With sentences you run the risk of reading them and thus stifling your presentation effectiveness.

The best alternative for completing the final draft is to use short phrases that convey just enough meaning to keep you on track but that are not long enough for you to begin reading them as part of your presentation. Feel free, however, to write out any grabber or memorable statements that you want to make sure you use. These tend to be panic points so having them written will add to your sense of security.

Once your speech is in final draft and you have practiced it at least three times, check to see if your speech passes the 5 Cs. Is it:

- Clear?
- Complete?
- Concise?
- Concrete?
- Correct?

Your preparation isn't complete until you have covered each of these Cs.

# 8

# KNOWING YOUR
# AUDIENCE

*You must look into people,
as well as at them.*
*—Lord Chesterfield*

To relate your speech effectively to the audience, you need to know who they are. Once you know who they are, you can use that knowledge to select a subject that interests and accommodates as many of them as you can.

Whether you speak to a large or a small group, study your audience in advance to determine how they may feel and think about you and your subject. Each audience will be different.

## STATUS OF AUDIENCE

Why is the audience assembled? Are they required to be present or is it voluntary? If you will be the keynote speaker at a convention with 1200 registrants from across the United States, who either paid their own way or had their companies cover the registration and hotel fees, who are all employed in the same industry, and this is an awards banquet, then you have a great deal of information to go on.

Members of such an audience are probably glad to be attending and are likely to be receptive to you and your ideas. You can easily find out characteristics of the audience, since they are all in the same industry.

Conversely, if you are giving an informal talk to company employees on the topic "Meeting Deadlines," you may need to do more digging for details to find out their various working conditions, and whether they chose to come or their bosses caused them to attend.

## SIZE

Next to incorrectly identifying an audience's knowledge about a particular subject, speakers tell the most horror stories about misjudging the size of their audience.

The size of your audience affects many elements of your speech. If you prepare for an audience of 35, and 100 people attend, you won't have enough handouts and your visuals may be too small to see. Always bring additional copies of any handout materials you plan to use. Also, bring the original so that extra copies can be made at the last minute, if necessary.

Knowing the audience size will determine the room setup and the types of visual aids to use.

## DEMOGRAPHICS

Demographics, which are characteristics of audiences such as age, education, occupation, and socioeconomic status, will impact on the way you use language and examples, and on the way you frame your main points and illustrate them. Information about religion, cultural/ethnic breakdowns, political affiliation and group membership can also be of value to your preparation.

In a business situation, you need to know which areas of the company will be represented in your audience. Will the sales and marketing vice president be there? How will her needs for information be different from the applications development specialist who will also be attending? Can you direct specific portions of your presentation to their individual needs?

If I were going to speak about fire safety to a packed community center, it would be useful to know if the area has a large population of elderly people. If that were the case, I would direct my examples to specific fire safety problems of the elderly, such as wearing long robes while working at the stove, which is a fire hazard, or using knitted pot holders to hold hot cooking utensils (knit materials do not prevent heat from passing through).

## AUDIENCE ATTITUDES

Demographic data about your audience, information about their feelings toward you, your speech, the occasion, and your purpose, can directly affect your chances for success. There are five basic types of audience: favorable, uninformed, apathetic, mixed, and hostile.

### The Favorable Audience

On occasion, you will talk to people who support either you personally or your attitude and beliefs. For example, you may be a known expert on management training, heart transplants, or child-rearing, and the people who come to hear you speak have read your book or followed your public successes on television talk shows.

While you can't take a supportive audience for granted, you can assume areas of agreement. Since you don't have to spend time convincing the audience that you are credible and your ideas are sound, you have more flexibility calling the favorable audience to action.

If I were speaking to an audience of business leaders about supporting a candidate who wanted to cut business taxes, I would plan my speech differently than if I were speaking to a group of union members about the same candidate. With the favorable audience, I would spend most of the time talking about specific ways people could show their support and mobilize others to act.

## The Uninformed Audience

When people are unfamiliar with a topic, they attempt to associate it with something they know. They will probably have no preconceived attitude toward the subject. In this situation, your goal is to inform your audience so they will understand this new information.

A county health director I know developed an effective way to get her audiences to listen and understand. When she began speaking about AIDS to community audiences in the mid-1980s, she would first explain the high statistics of teenage pregnancy and venereal disease. These were familiar areas with which audience members could relate.

By the time she worked her way into the subject of AIDS, they could make the connection between all these sexually transmitted diseases, and it was easier for them to accept the possibility of AIDS invading their community.

## The Apathetic Audience

One task of the speaker is to influence persons who are indifferent or who don't care to become involved. Study your audience carefully to determine the nature of their indifference.

For example, you may be explaining a new company benefit to employees. If it's a specific benefit, such as paternity leave, it may not interest anyone except married men in their child-producing years.

If possible, speak to the person arranging your presentation to see if the audience can be narrowed down to those interested in your topic. You may have little or no control over who is invited; in those cases, search for a connection between the audience and the subject matter. Using the preceding example, I might talk about how instituting paternity leave may indicate a shift in social attitudes or in company policy about all types of benefits.

Conversely, you may have a broad and complicated subject, such as employee stock option plans and be speaking to an audience that is diverse in its knowledge of the plan—some would be impatient with a step-by-step explanation, and others confused by a detailed question-and-answer session.

Several options are available for handling audiences with differing levels of knowledge about your topic. If the majority of people are not knowledgeable, I use experts in the audience to help me explain certain points. This makes the experts feel good about themselves yet also keeps them on their toes and interested in the presentation. After all, they never know when I may call on them for assistance.

If a minority of the audience knows nothing about a subject and the rest have a moderate amount of expertise, I gear my speech to the majority and offer to talk to individuals during breaks or at lunch to give them the background they need to use the information.

## The Mixed Audience

There are two types of mixed audiences: the mixed favorable and the mixed hostile. The mixed favorable includes favorable, uninformed, and apathetic members. Although this type of audience is not difficult, it is important to remember to take the time to inform the uninformed and create the WIIFT for the apathetic. One hostile person in the audience can poison the whole bag of apples and create a mixed hostile audience. One hostile person can introduce information that could shift the minds of the entire group. Prepare for a hostile audience and you will be ready for any mixed group.

## The Hostile Audience

At times you may address audiences who are hostile either to you, your position on a topic, or both. When approaching a hostile audience, begin with a friendly position—look for areas of agreement. Try to establish yourself as an honorable person.

Attempt to learn why they are hostile. Without understanding their hostility, you will never be able to address it. Answer the audience's objections to you or your proposal with valid reasons and reliable information. I can think of no better example than that of First Lady Barbara Bush, when she gave a commencement address at Wellesley College.

Mrs. Bush faced at least a partially hostile audience of graduates who wore purple arm bands to protest her selection as commencement speaker, when their choice had been novelist Alice Walker, author of *The Color Purple*. This hostile faction had protested because they claimed Barbara Bush was selected on the basis of her husband's accomplishments and not her own.

Barbara Bush answered that protest with a frank and open speech that was not berating, but simply stated her position and expressed positive hopes for them in making their mark as graduates of the college. She won great praise for her speech not only from the graduates attending the commencement but from media commentators across the country.

Suppose the person you want to reach, the ultimate decision maker, is not in the audience, and someone from the audience is reporting back to that decision maker. You will want to arm the messenger with all the facts that would be needed to provide a WIIFT from the decision maker's point of view. If possible, meet with that person one-on-one after the group presentation. Ask if there are any concerns about presenting the information to the decision maker. Mention that you will be available if needed to make the presentation or to answer questions.

## *WHEN TO GATHER YOUR INFORMATION*

An effective speaker gathers audience data before, during, and after the speech.

- *Before a Speech.* Your best sources for information about your audience will be the meeting organizer. Also, you may have prior experience with or knowledge about the audience. Ask people you know about the audience, get in touch with people who have addressed the same audience before, or read literature that the organization produces. Research recent issues of the local newspaper for stories on the organization or group. For business presentations, talk to others in the corporation including secretaries and colleagues.

Just before the speech, arrive early enough to review any last-minute details and meet members of your audience.

- *During Your Speech.* Your best source of data will be the nonverbal, and sometimes verbal, cues given by the audience. If they are laughing at your humor and applauding at the right moments, you definitely have their attention and are reaching them. If it isn't working, be flexible, do something different. If people are talking to one another, or getting up to leave the room, you will readily perceive that you have a hostile audience on your hands. Since you will have prepared for a hostile audience you will be ready to handle the group. Realistically, the verbal and nonverbal cues usually will fall somewhere in between.

- *After a Speech.* Remain a few minutes after your speech to see if anyone approaches you with further questions. If not, make the first gesture and ask some audience members what they thought about the substance of your presentation. You could also hand out an informal one-page survey such as the one on the next page.

If you want the names, addresses, and/or phone numbers of audience members who would like more information from you, this sheet is a good place to request that information.

I have known CPR (cardiopulmonary resuscitation) instructors who used a quiz to gauge how much their course participants had learned from their presentation before moving to hands-on practice on mannequins and the awarding of certification. They also distributed a quick one-page survey so that course participants could rate the instructors on their approach and effectiveness as speakers.

This kind of simple follow-up can really help, not only if you speak to a similar group, but in all your subsequent presentations. The more you speak, and the more you learn, the better speaker you will become.

## PRESENTATION FEEDBACK SHEET

Please take a minute to check either Yes or No for each of the questions below. Your responses will help us plan our next presentation.

| *Presentation* | *Yes* | *No* |
|---|---|---|
| Covered the right amount of material? | _____ | _____ |
| Content was relevant? | _____ | _____ |
| Time allocations were appropriate? | _____ | _____ |
| Difficulty level of material was appropriate? | _____ | _____ |
| Sequence of sessions facilitated learning? | _____ | _____ |

| *Visual Aids/Printed Materials* | | |
|---|---|---|
| Technically accurate? | _____ | _____ |
| Up to date? | _____ | _____ |
| Well organized? | _____ | _____ |
| Relevant? | _____ | _____ |
| Good quality? | _____ | _____ |
| Complete? | _____ | _____ |

| *Speaker* | | |
|---|---|---|
| Enthusiastic? | _____ | _____ |
| Knowledgeable? | _____ | _____ |
| Understandable? | _____ | _____ |
| Interesting? | _____ | _____ |
| Helpful? | _____ | _____ |

**Thanks for your help!**

# 9

# *ANALYZING YOUR AUDIENCE*

*Never ignore a gut feeling,
but never believe that it's
enough.*
> *—Robert Heller*

As we saw in the last chapter, it is essential to know who your audience is ahead of time. Just as conditioning, exercise, and practice pay off in other sports, your extra efforts in learning about your audience will pay off in the audience-centered sport of giving presentations. Answering the following 18 questions will help enormously when you actually make your presentation:

## 1. How Many People Will Attend?

The size of your audience determines to a great extent, how you will select your topic and practice your speech. If the group is large, you may need to choose a grabber statement in your introduction and a memorable statement in your conclusion that are more universal than you would choose for a smaller, more intimate group. If the group is small, you would not have to practice certain elements of your delivery, such as tape-recording yourself as you project your voice to the back rows of the room.

Reinforcing a key point in the previous chapter, you do not want surprises—5 people in a classroom when you were expecting 40, or 1500 people in a coliseum when you thought you were addressing a small break-out group of 75. Don't assume anything! Talk to the conference or meeting coordinator, or the person in charge of admissions, to find out the exact number of your group.

## 2. Is the Presentation Designed to Accommodate the Expected Audience Size?

Most meeting, conference, or school program coordinators are aware of their responsibilities for making sure the room in which you are speaking is set up with a podium, a microphone, slide projector, VCR monitor, overhead projector, and either a chalkboard or flipchart.

They may not be aware of your basic needs, however, unless you inform them in advance. You may have to make your own arrangements. If you are unusually short or tall, for example, the microphone may need special adjustments. If your visuals are slides, you will need a projector, screen, and someone to dim the lights at your cue, as well as a small light on the lectern or podium, so that you can read your outline. The variations are endless. Write a list of your needs, and *make sure* that it is communicated to the event coordinator. Then arrive early to ensure everything is set up to your satisfaction.

Any experienced speaker can rattle off details of at least three or four instances when she had to handle some last-minute predicaments that someone else might have fixed. I have no sympathy for speakers who arrive only a few minutes before giving their presentations and discover a problem; they deserve it.

## 3. What Is the Occasion for the Presentation?

Knowing the occasion or circumstances will help you frame your topic. If it is a company's 50th anniversary, then your talk about productivity in the 1990s can take on a historic perspective.

If your talk on environmental hazards in the workplace takes place three days after a dangerously high level of lead is found in the drinking water of a major corporation's headquarters, then you will want to use the newsworthy event while calling company leaders to action.

If your audience of blue-collar workers has been forced to assemble and has no idea that your talk is to be about cutbacks and layoffs, then you need to plan time for a question-and-answer period. If you feel you may not know the answers to all possible questions, have the experts on hand who can help you.

### 4. How Old Are Members of the Audience?

The age distribution of your audience is a key factor in the selection of your topic and the examples or illustrations you choose. If you are drawing on "Howdy Doody" and "Sky King," two 1950s television shows for young people, as examples for an audience of college-age students, they may not understand the reference because they were born long after those shows aired.

Likewise, if you refer to *New Kids on the Block* or *Whitesnake* (current rock music groups), you may draw blank looks from the over-50 crowd. If the age distribution of your audience is wide, and your subject is the U.S. space program, to appeal to all elements of the audience, you may want to talk about the contributions of the early space program, and about future projects, such as the proposed space station.

### 5. What Is the Gender Distribution of Your Audience?

The gender distribution of your audience will determine your approach to such topics as alternative treatments for breast cancer, treatment of testicular cancer, working mothers and child care, and how to be a Big Brother. All such subjects are gender specific.

Using the example of a general subject—the space program—again, if a large number of women are in the audience, you might supplement the subject with a look at women's increasing contributions to the program.

## 6. What Is the Educational Level of Your Audience?

Knowing your audience's educational level will help you decide how to express your subject in terms that everyone understands. As an obvious comparison, if you are speaking to high school dropouts about fire safety, you may want to concentrate on one aspect, such as the "stop, drop, and roll" drill to save someone who is on fire. If you are talking to graduate students in emergency planning, you will be able to cover more sophisticated, technical points.

## 7. What Occupations Are Represented?

It may not be as easy to scout out your audience's occupations, unless you are speaking to a specific convention of dentists or bankers, or if you are able to get a copy of an organization's roster, such as a Rotary club, that shows a listing of occupations along with names.

It may be useful to mingle and talk with people in the audience before you speak to get a feel for occupations. The most blatant errors, such as favoring tree conservation before a congregation of printers, can be prevented by a little preinvestigation.

## 8. What Is the Socioeconomic Status of Your Audience?

Speaking on tax shelters to an audience of middle- to low-income wage earners is a mistake you could make if you do not look into the socioeconomic status of your audience before you speak. However, there are tax concerns for each level of status, so with investigation beforehand, you can gear your presentation to any level.

## 9. What Religions Are Represented?

You would not want to talk about Western fashion to a group of Muslim women, or the issue of pro-choice to Catholic parishioners or fundamental Christian groups. It helps to know the religions of your audience before you select your topic, but it is not always an easy question to ask, as many people are sensitive about discussing religion. Your best preparation is to be as objective as possible when covering a subject that might be sensitive to certain religions.

## 10. What Cultural or Ethnic Groups Are Represented?

Understanding cultural or ethnic differences is a very helpful tool in selecting and limiting your topic. For example, if your subject is how to break into show business and the majority of your audience is African American, then you would need to highlight in your speech the opportunities that African Americans have experienced in trying to get work in Hollywood and how they can overcome existing barriers.

If you are speaking on the same topic to an elderly group of men and women in a posh community retirement home, you might speak of the obstacles faced by Kirk Douglas, Bette Davis, or Humphrey Bogart.

## 11. What Political Affiliations Are Represented?

If your audience is of a specific political party, then your speech may be framed by or play on the viewpoints of that party. If your audience is a mixture of political affiliations, then try to show as many different political viewpoints that relate to your subject as possible. For example, a college audience today could represent both far left and far right political viewpoints.

## 12. What Organizations Are Represented?

It would be helpful to know if your audience belongs to certain groups, such as the American Medical Association or the American Bar Association, so that perhaps one of your anecdotes or examples could play on the latest headline from that group. If several members belong to a local group, use at least one anecdote or example that draws their attention.

## 13. What Is the Audience's Attitude Toward You?

Mingling with your audience before your speech can help you find out how they feel about you—whether they know who you are, if they have read your book or heard you speak before. Are their opinions shaped by what they have read in the media about you, or do they speak to you in an open and nonjudgmental manner? By learning the audience's perception of you, you will know whether to take the defensive or offensive in your presentation.

## 14. Do You Know Your Audience's Attitudes Toward Your Subject?

If you are about to speak to your staff about doing a better job because a project is going poorly, you especially need to grasp your audience's attitudes toward the talk you are about to give. If they feel browbeaten already and morale is low because they know the project is going badly, then it makes no sense in your speech to beat them down more for doing a bad job.

If they are unconcerned about the quality of their work, then you need to do some cheerleading and remind them of the purpose of the project. Instill pride in their work and an enthusiasm about rolling up their shirtsleeves and tackling the task anew. Connect them to their vision and commitment to serve on this project.

If your audience is unaware of any problem on the project, then you need to do some eye-opening and put forth some frank bottom-line figures.

## 15. What Is the Attitude About the Subject Matter?

Do you know if your audience will be neutral, friendly, hostile, or apathetic? Have you made any plans to handle their attitudes? Going one step further, talk to members of your audience before your speech as recommended earlier, to get a feel for their mood, from friendly to hostile. If they are hostile, they may not have the willingness to listen to what you are going to say. Hence, your grabber statement will have to be a shocker, something totally different from what they expected to hear. Then, you will need to build some bridges of understanding before launching into your topic.

If your audience is friendly, don't put them on the defensive by unnecessarily riling them. I recall a speech a pediatrician gave as part of a prenatal education program at a hospital. Her audience was a cheerful group of expectant parents. Unfortunately when she began the subject of breastfeeding, she said, "Of course, all of you are going to breast-feed, I hope," which set off a chorus of irate stares, rustling papers, coughing, and whispering among those parents who had chosen to formula-feed. Her judgmental opening created defensive walls that need not have existed.

### 16. What Is Your Systematic Plan for Gathering Data about Your Audience Before You Speak?

On a sheet of paper, brainstorm all the possible sources of information about your audience, from the coordinators of the event at which you will speak, to obtaining publications put out by the group that you will address. You can continue to gather data up until the time of your speech by arriving early and talking to members of your audience as they gather before the event. Write out your strategy to collect your data.

### 17. How Will You Observe Your Audience's Reactions During Your Speech?

Decide before you give your speech what you will be looking for, from reactions to your humorous anecdotes, to whether people are reading their programs as you speak or nodding their heads in rapt attention. To maintain an audience-centered focus once you have begun your speech, your attention should be on your audience and not on your outline.

### 18. What Is Your Plan for Gathering Any Reactions from Your Audience after Your Speech?

You could use the sample from the last chapter or jot down 10 specific questions to ask your audience. Look at the questions and determine how the answers would help you improve your future presentations.

Once you have your final questions, hand them out at your speech. If the talk is informal, stay after the speech and mingle with your audience to determine their reactions to what you have said.

---

### AUDIENCE ANALYSIS CHECKLIST

1. How many people will attend?
2. Is the presentation designed to accommodate the expected audience size?
3. What is the occasion for the presentation?
4. How old are members of the audience?
5. What is the gender distribution?
6. What is the educational level?
7. What occupations are represented?
8. What is the socioeconomic status of the audience?
9. What religions are represented?
10. What cultures or ethnic groups are represented?
11. What political affiliations are represented?
12. What organizations are represented?
13. What is the audience's attitude toward you?
14. What is the attitude about the subject?
15. What is the attitude about the subject matter?
16. What is your plan to gather data before you speak?
17. How will you observe your audience's reactions during your speech?

# PART THREE

# WORKING ON YOUR PRESENTATION

*WHAT'S IN IT FOR YOU*

In Chapter 10, you'll learn how to outline your presentation. The correct format for an outline, methods of outlining, and sample outlines are included. Reading the material on the basic outline of a speech, transitioning, and the criteria for eliminating parts will help you create a logical, easy-to-follow presentation that covers just the right amount of information for your audience.

An introduction sets the stage. In Chapter 11, you'll learn how to grab the audience's attention and let them know what's in it for them (WIIFT) so your message has the most impact. Establishing your credibility will help your audience buy your message; after reading this chapter, you'll know all the vital pieces of an introduction.

To organize the body of your presentation, you'll want to check out Chapter 12. Choose the best order for your subject, understand internal summaries, and you will be well on your way to having your audience understand and remember your message.

Developing your supporting materials is covered in Chapter 13 where you will learn how to substantiate your point of view, clarify your information, and involve your audience.

The final part of your speech, the conclusion, is easy to ruin if you have not planned how you will tie together all the pieces you have presented. You'll need to review your main points and make a memorable statement so the audience retains your message; Chapter 14 shows you how.

You can make the perfect speech and be ready to head out the door on a high when, wham, you are hit with a tough question. In Chapter 15, you'll learn how to maintain your credibility by the way in which you respond to questions. If you follow the checklist for making the most of your Q&A session, you'll have nothing to fear.

# 10

# *THE OUTLINE*

*The great artists and
thinkers are simplifiers.*
*—Henri Frederic Aniel*

**A**n outline is to a speech what a blueprint is to a house, a chart is to a cruise, and an agenda is to a meeting. An outline ensures that your speech has form, direction, and includes the points you want to make.

> An outline is a tool for planning. It is a visual representation of ideas and data through which you inform, persuade, or entertain your audience.

If you are following the 10 steps for preparing your presentation, explained in Chapter 7, then you have already drafted your basic three to five main points and will use them subsequently as a springboard for writing your introduction and conclusion. The task of outlining your speech in final draft form comes before the introduction and conclusion; the latter are best handled after the body of your speech has been prepared.

## *REASONS FOR USING STANDARD PAPER*

As discussed in Chapter 7, I recommend that in outlining your speech you use standard 8 1/2- by 11-inch paper rather than note cards. If you use three or four note cards for each sheet of paper, by the time you have 16 note cards, they will become too unwieldy. If you flip the note cards, they may get out of order. A few sheets of standard size paper will serve you well.

Outline your speech rather than write it out—when you write a speech word for word you tend to read it. Remember, reading diminishes your rapport with the audience. Writing out your speech is also like wearing a straitjacket: You are strapped into it without having the freedom to adapt to the audience or other speakers. Speaking from an outline allows you to be spontaneous and organized.

## METHODS OF OUTLINING

The following sections explain why you should stay away from either the single-word outline or the whole-sentence outline.

### Single-Word Outline

If you use a single word to represent an entire train of thought, it is easy to forget the many ideas behind that one word. A key word may have meant something to you when you prepared and practiced your speech at home, but now, up in front of all those people, under the stress of the moment, it may not mean a thing.

The single word outline uses a key word for each section of the outline. This method is barren in detail, and its usefulness is limited. This sample illustrates a single-word outline using a portion of the phrase outline presented later in this chapter:

    II. Body
       A. Need
          1. Half
          2. 4th
          3. $800

B. Works
   1. Goals
   2. Objectives
     a. Do
     b. Show
     c. Level

## Sentence Outline

The opposite problem occurs with whole sentence outlines. The more you write out, the more you will read. The more you read, the more your attention will be focused on your paper and not on your audience. Also there is a difference between oral and written language. Oral language is simpler with incomplete and shorter sentences.

The sentence outline is written entirely with complete sentences. This format is not useful since many speakers will succumb to the temptation to read the outline word for word. This example is a sentence outline:

II. Body
   A. We need guaranteed learning for the following three reasons.
     1. First, half the students who enter college drop out sometime during the first year. They never become sophomores.
     2. Some teenagers graduate from high school with only a fourth-grade reading level.
     3. Although we spend an average of more than $800 per year for each student, we still have no assurance of what that money will produce.
   B. Guaranteed learning works if the following four steps are used, etc. . . .

## Phrase Outline

Phrases make the ideal outline. They are just long enough to jog your memory and short enough for a jump-off point, so that your attention is on your audience, and not on your outline.

Most points of the outline are written as phrases, although grabber statements, transitions, and other memorable statements can
be written in full. The phrase gives more detail; therefore, its usefulness is increased. The following example uses mostly phrases;
is organized into an introduction, a body with three main points,
and a conclusion; and lists the audience and the purpose of the
speech at the top.

Audience:           New York School Board Association
Speech Purpose:  After hearing my speech, the audience will agree
                 that schools should guarantee their instruction.

    I.   Introduction (grabber, WIIFT, source credibility, and
        preview)
        A. Would you buy a brand X car if you knew that half of
           those cars broke down in one year or less?
        B. As a school board association, we are concerned that we
           provide a quality education for each student.
        C. As a member of the community and the school board I
           too am concerned about our students and their ability to
           contribute to our society.
        D. Schools to guarantee their instruction.

   II.   Body
        A. The need for guaranteed learning:
          1. Half of students who enter college never become
            sophomores.
          2. Some graduate from high school with only a fourth-
            grade reading level.
          3. We spend an average of more than $800 per year per
            student, yet have no assurance of what that money
            will produce.

TRANSITION: We can guarantee learning when we understand
how it works.

        B. How guaranteed learning works—four steps:
          1. Community and school set broad goals.
          2. Teacher establishes specific, measurable objectives,
            stating:
            a. What the student is to do to show he has learned.
            b. How he is to show it—conditions.
            c. Level he is to achieve.

      3. Teacher then designs instruction to attain those objectives.

      4. Teacher tests effectiveness of instruction, redesigns to ensure that learning occurs.

TRANSITION: There are successful examples of these guaranteed learning agreements in our community.

    C. Success of guaranteed learning:

      1. Gary, Indiana: entire K-5 school, 400 students

      2. More than 200 projects across country.

III. Conclusion (review and memorable statement)

    A. Guaranteed learning to be provided by all schools:

      1. It is needed.

      2. It is a clear, specific 4-step process.

      3. It works!

    B. Guarantees exist for cars, orange juice, chicken, cough drops, dishwashers, a wide variety of our products—why not education?

## OUTLINING TIPS

1. *Write Your Purpose.* At the top of your outline, write your specific purpose. It will serve as a reminder of what you expect to accomplish.

2. *Don't Be Too Short.* Your outline needs to be long enough and detailed enough to remind you of the ideas, points, and data you are to present.

3. *Don't Be Too Long.* Your outline is not to be a manuscript. The more you write, the more you will read, and draw attention away from your audience.

4. *Don't Be Too General.* Simple, brief, generalized subject headings have little value. The outline is a crutch, so make it worthwhile.

5. *Don't Overstructure.* Don't make your outline too involved or overstructured. You may get lost in its nooks and crannies, especially if there is a time crunch and you are in the middle of a maze. The outline needs to be simple enough

that you know what you want to say at a glance, yet have enough information to help you if you get stuck.

6. *Highlight Your Key Phrases*. Use a pink or blue highlighter to make your key phrases stand out on your outline. Don't use a yellow highlighter because yellow is difficult to see under fluorescent lighting.

## THE THREE MAIN PARTS OF YOUR SPEECH

Whether outlining, or actually delivering your speech, consider that most speeches can be organized with an introduction, body, and conclusion. The *introduction* is the most important part because you have to capture the attention of your audience, and

---

### BASIC FORMAT OF A SPEECH

I.  Introduction (tell *what* you are going to tell them).

   A. Grabber statement: Get attention.

   B. WIIFT (What's In It For Them).

   C. Source credibility: What qualifies you to speak on this subject.

   D. Preview: Road map of where you are going.

TRANSITION

II.  Body (tell them).

   A. Three to five main points (with transitions connecting each point).

     1. Arrange logically.

     2. Support with data.

TRANSITION

III.  Conclusion (tell what you have told them).

   A. Review.

   B. Memorable statement.

you need to preview what you are going to say. The introduction constitutes about 10 to 15 percent of your total speech. So if you're speaking for 30 minutes, your introduction would be roughly 3 minutes in duration.

The *body* of the speech is organized to accomplish your purpose to inform or persuade. Use your three to five main points, and support them with various types of data, using transitions to connect your materials. The body constitutes 70 to 80 percent of your speech.

The *conclusion* is like beautiful wrapping paper on a gift—it's the final detail that ties up your speech with a review and a memorable statement. The conclusion constitutes about 5 to 10 percent of your speech.

## MAKING A SMOOTH TRANSITION

To move smoothly through your speech, you write transitional phrases in the margins of your outline. Transitional phrases are short comments that will carry you from the introduction to the body of your speech, and from the body to the conclusion.

You also will need transitional phrases to move you to other main points within the body of your speech. This will keep you from saying "uh, um" or pausing awkwardly as you move from one part of your presentation to the next. A good transition is an internal summary, such as, "Now that you know . . . ," "With this in mind let's look at . . . ," or "We can move on to the next point, which is . . ."

## PREDETERMINING WHAT CAN BE ELIMINATED

Ask yourself the following question: "What MUST, SHOULD, COULD the audience know about my subject?" Color code these sections on your outline so you know immediately which section to eliminate if you have to cut 15 minutes. You also may want to color-code your visual aides for MUST, SHOULD, and COULD. If you use slides stored in a tray, always mark the slides that *must* be shown; then in a time crunch, you will be able to pull out the nonessential slides.

On your outline, put a box around the area or areas of your speech that you can do without, so that if time is running short, you can eliminate the most appropriate section. I have seen speakers talk faster to get everything in. Watching their speeded-up motions and listening to their words rush over each other, I become nervous. I'm so busy hoping they won't stumble that I completely lose track of whatever they are trying to say.

Speeches almost always run longer than you anticipate so prepare your speech for 75% of the time you have been allotted. Even then, indicate the material that can be cut if the need arises. If you prepare for the possibility of a time crunch, you will handle the elimination process much more smoothly.

Using another color put a box around what you want to make sure you tell the audience, and what you'd like to tell them, time permitting. These measures help you in prioritizing your information; color code these boxes for more clarity.

## *THE PROPER FORMAT FOR AN OUTLINE*

Two additional suggestions when outlining will help you keep the audience at the center of your attention. To make your outline easy to read, I recommend typing it in bold print, using a 14-point type on a word processor or computer; if your notes are handwritten, use a medium point felt-tip pen in blue or black ink. That way, you can move a few steps away and still see your outline. Also, type only on the top two thirds of each page. That keeps your chin up and your voice from falling. Use the planning sheet for preparation but not to read from during your presentation.

An outline, even a good one, will not guarantee results. The value is that it ensures that you'll have a logical presentation of the points and data in your speech.

# 11

# THE INTRODUCTION

*The beginning is the most*
*important part of the work.*
*—Plato*

*Look with favor upon a*
*bold beginning.*
*—Virgil*

A strong introduction is vital to the success of your talk because it can win over your audience immediately. The introduction serves four main purposes:

- It focuses the audience's attention.
- It establishes WIIFT (what's in it for them).
- It establishes you as a credible source.
- It previews your subject.

## FOCUSING THE AUDIENCE'S ATTENTION

Without the attention and interest of your audience, you cannot accomplish your purpose to inform or persuade them. Your challenge is to make the audience want to listen. How?

A *grabber* statement is a hook, a way to pull the audience's attention into what you are going to tell them. It can be a story, a real or hypothetical question, a statistic, or a humorous anecdote. It can be any of those things, but it's best if it's your first words and grabs your audience's attention.

Kay Koplovitz, president and CEO of USA Network says, "I try to start with a controversial statement to grab attention. People will always hold out to see how on earth you're going to support it." In addition to Ms. Koplovitz's idea, the following are examples of the kinds of grabber statements you can use in your speeches.

## 1. Ask a Question

If your speech is about drug use in the workplace, then you may want to shock the audience as to the relevance of your subject by asking a series of point-blank and specific questions:

> Do you use drugs in the workplace?
>
> Do you know of anyone who uses drugs in the workplace?

The questions are sure to set off a search in people's minds for someone they know who uses drugs. You may, with a different subject, want to pose a hypothetical question, to get your audience to think, such as:

> Are you aware that, with the proper data, your marketing decisions can easily be made?
>
> If you had your life to live over again, what would you do differently?
>
> If your department were given a million dollars, what would you change?

## 2. State an Unusual Fact

If your subject is the high instance of student absenteeism in high schools, you may want to begin your talk with a statistic, such as this one:

> Forty percent of today's teenagers are being brought up in single-parent homes.

If your subject is the quality of programming on network television, you might want to cite the following statistic:

On this day, more people see a typical television sitcom than have seen all of the stage performances of Shakespeare's plays in all of the more than 400 years since he wrote them.

### 3. Give an Illustration, Example, or Story

Calling a vivid image to the minds of your audience is an excellent way to grab their attention and make the content real for each listener. You can do that by painting a picture through a story or illustration that relates to your subject. For example, if your subject is ethics, you can say:

> Last night I was walking home from the library when I noticed a woman's purse lying on the sidewalk. As I leaned over to pick it up . . .

> To no one else's knowledge, I accidentally dented someone's car in a parking lot on Tuesday . . .

Using stories that happened to you makes the content yours.

### 4. Present a Quotation

Everyone likes a catchy phrase or quote. In this day of coffee mugs, T-shirts, wall plaques, and daily calendars all offering quips and quotes, the device is one that will be welcomed in a speech, if it relates well to your subject and has not been overused.

During the first year of George Bush's administration, for instance, far too many speakers quoted the President's "read my lips . . ." quip, and it quickly became overworked. Quotations by famous people can be found in the reference section of your local library.

The chapter-opening quotes in this book, for example, could all be used as grabber statements (e.g., "Mark Twain once said . . .").

### 5. Refer to a Historic Event

Important anniversaries of historic events happen every day. Some newspapers across the country carry items such as "Today in History," where you can pick up such tidbits of information.

You can arouse the interest of your audience and perhaps trigger a memory if you say, for example,

> On this day, more than 25 years ago, the United States . . .

## 6. Use Humor

Humor is an age-old device for establishing rapport with the audience through the bond of shared human experience. The key criterion for using humor is to make sure you are comfortable with it, it is in good taste, it is relevant to your speech, and it is funny. For example, when giving seminars on powerful presentation skills I like to start off with:

> The human brain is a wonderful thing. It operates from the moment you're born until the first time you get up to make a speech.

## 7. Get the Audience Talking to You and Each Other

Depending on the number of people in the audience, the purpose of the speech, and the characteristics of the audience members, you may want to have people introduce themselves or make an opening comment. There are several reasons to have participants introduce themselves.

At a meeting of government contractors, for instance, some in the audience may feel constrained from asking questions until they know the names of the companies (who may be potential competitors) that other audience members work for.

When time allows, the participants' introductions allow you to establish rapport with the audience by commenting on the information they volunteer. It also gives other audience members a chance to establish linkages for later conversations and networking.

Whenever possible, I ask participants to give their name, their company, and the reason they came to the presentation. Even if I have done my homework investigating the audience before the speech, such information is a valuable addition I can use as I speak.

Once you have gained your audience's attention, you need to design a way to get from your grabber statement to your preview.

This transition need only be a phrase or a sentence where you suggest the relationship between your opening and your preview. Here are a few examples:

That true story illustrates the need for the new tax proposal I want to suggest to you tonight.

This example demonstrates that management training is vital to the development of our human resources.

Those are the shocking facts of what is happening in some hospitals; now what can be done about them? Let me offer some suggestions.

## WHAT'S IN IT FOR YOUR AUDIENCE?

Not every audience member is going to be receptive to your speech. And if they are resistant, you cannot always inform or persuade them. They may have been told to attend your presentation by their boss, or are in your class for the credit only. Every member of your audience is asking: What's in this for me? Your job is to let them know as quickly as possible so they will be motivated to listen. You have only your introduction to get the attention of your audience; if the grabber didn't do it, then establish clearly WIIFT.

You might compliment them as subject matter experts, or impress upon them the critical nature of the information you are about to present. You want to say something that will get them past the initial resistance, peak their interest, and establish a rapport between you and your audience.

Sometimes people at conferences sign up for workshops, but if bored, they move from room to room until they find a session that interests them. If someone leaves, keep in mind that he could be leaving for a dozen different reasons and that you still have the rest of the audience with you. Focus your energy on your listeners.

## ESTABLISH YOUR CREDIBILITY

Talk about yourself in terms of your background and expertise in relation to the subject you will be discussing. Of course, if you are

part of the group and everyone knows you, or if someone introduces you, you don't need to discuss your background. Do ensure
that your audience knows you are an expert.

Sometimes, I begin my talk by saying, "Throughout my 26 years
of teaching people to speak . . . ." When I attend presentations
where organizers spend five minutes rattling off the speaker's degrees and published books, I expect the person to be fantastic
when he or she finally gets up to speak. If the presentation is any
less than that, I resent all the time given to building up the cre-
dentials. Most audiences appreciate real-world experiences and
knowledge more than degrees, honors, and memberships in dues-
paying associations.

Talk to the person who will be introducing you to discover what
he or she plans to say or provide a written introduction as you'd
like it. Then plan your opening statement around that information.

It is a mistake to assume that your introducer will know what to
say about you. I once observed the introducer get so excited about
the content he had heard the last time the presenter spoke that he
practically gave the speech. When the speaker got to the podium,
her main points had been covered by the introducer but the audience knew nothing about the speaker's background. If you have
time, practice with your introducer—the payoff will be worth it.

## PREVIEW THE SUBJECT

You can help your audience understand the logic and the direction
of where you are going in your speech by previewing the subject.
Remember, they do not have a road map. Lead them where you
want them to go in a clear, specific, and precise manner. Here are
some techniques for previewing your subject:

### State the Purpose of Your Speech

If your purpose is to inform, tell your audience what you mean to
accomplish. It is best when this is very brief and direct. For example, you might say:

I want to talk with you about the problem of waste in the welfare program.

Or, you might say:

My question is this: How can taxes be reduced?

If your goal is to persuade your audience do not tell them in the beginning—instead build your reasoning as you move through your content.

### List the Main Points of Your Speech

To be even more specific, relate the three to five main points that you will cover in the body of your speech. In other words, tell them what you are going to tell them. For example:

Travel is good because it is educational, economical, and memorable.

Or, you might say:

My candidate has four advantages: One, she's experienced; two, she's creative; three, she's qualified; and four, she's understanding.

## SOME DO'S AND DON'TS FOR INTRODUCING YOUR SPEECH

You don't have to offer the four parts of your introduction in order except for the grabber statement—it comes first. This may seem to be a lot to fit into an introduction that is only 10 to 15 percent of your speech. However, the introduction is critical. It is your job, as you start to speak, to turn that daydreaming, diverse group of individuals in front of you into a concentrating, stimulated, involved, thinking, and participating audience.

## DO'S AND DON'TS FOR INTRODUCTIONS

*Don'ts*

1. Don't apologize.

2. Don't be long-winded.

3. Don't antagonize or offend your audience.

4. Don't use irrelevant material.

5. Don't start with a trite phrase such as "Today, I'm going to talk about . . ."

6. Don't lead the audience to take a negative attitude toward your subject.

*Do's*

1. Do get the attention of the audience first—start with the grabber statement. In some instances, you may first give a brief greeting.

2. Do be confident in your attitude—step up with confidence; smile; speak out loudly and clearly; move with assurance; sound authoritative and pleasant; exude positive energy.

3. Do get set before you start to speak—once you've begun your speech, you don't want to arrange your notes, adjust the microphone, move the lectern, and so on.

4. Do be alert to tie in your grabber statement with the remarks of the previous speakers, other parts of the program, or with information given by the person who introduces you.

# 12

## *ORGANIZING THE BODY OF YOUR SPEECH*

*Begin at the beginning and go on till you come to the end; then stop.*
*—Lewis Carroll*

The body, or main text, of your speech develops the points that you previewed in your introduction. In developing these ideas, organize your materials in a way that the audience can easily follow. People have a need for logic; provide it by organizing your ideas so that your audience can understand. If you approach organizing as if it were a road map, you'll see that there are different paths you can take to get from the beginning to the end.

Your audience and your subject will determine which route you will take.

Public speaking is an audience-centered sport. When choosing your method of organization, consider your audience's needs.

# TYPES OF ORGANIZATION FOR INFORMATIVE SPEECHES

If the purpose of your speech is to inform your audience, the following types of organization are best for giving new information to your audience:

- Chronological order.
- Spatial order.
- Geographical order.
- Topical order.
- Comparison and contrast.
- Cause and effect.

## Chronological Order

A chronological speech is arranged in order of time of occurrence, or time sequence. If your subject covers how to follow the progress of a drug from inception through approval by the Federal Drug Administration, you might choose to explain the process using a time line as your outline.

A visual aid showing the time span, from start to finish, will help the audience see the big picture. If you use such a visual aid, refer to it periodically throughout the speech. Use it in the beginning and again as you describe each new step in the drug approval process.

## Spatial Order

A spatially organized speech pertains to the nature of space. For example, if your subject is how to set up point-of-purchase displays in a modern supermarket, you might explain the setup by describing the areas of the store that are involved, one by one. Again, visual aids will be of great use in helping people understand and remember the information you are giving them. If I were giving a talk about point-of-purchase displays, I would plan a demonstration. It need not be elaborate to get the points across.

I would borrow a cash register, place it on a counter, and put the different types of displays next to the register. Then people could see the strengths and weaknesses of each type for themselves. People retain *10 percent of what they read, 20 percent of what they hear, 30 percent of what they see, 50 percent of what they see and hear,* and *90 percent of what they see while doing.*

## Geographical Order

A geographically organized speech is also arranged by space, but as it specifically relates to geography. If your subject is the effects of the reunification of Germany, you could choose to start in Berlin and move geographically to Bonn. Maps would, of course, be useful here.

If the information on the map would be too small to see as a slide or overhead transparency, include a map in the handout package given to people as they register or check in.

## Topical Order

A topically organized speech takes a large topic and breaks it into several subtopics. If your subject is IBM, then your subtopics could be each type of software produced by the company. If your subject is the First Federal Bank you could discuss the four different types of loans offered by the bank.

## Comparison and Contrast

A speech organized by comparison and contrast compares characteristics, features, and qualities that are similar in two subjects and contrasts their differences. Comparison and contrast help clarify the unknown by referring to the known. For example, you might compare one bank's services with another bank's services, or contrast the city administration of one city against another city of similar population and budget.

People understand subjects better when the ideas are related to something they know on a personal level. Discussions about the deficit of the United States, for instance, can be overwhelming, unless your listeners have graduate degrees in economics. Most people cannot comprehend the numbers involved or how it all fits. Thus, if you compare the country's deficit with a household income, your audience will more easily comprehend the subject than if you discuss it as an abstract concept.

Our brain functions like a sponge or a rock depending on our openness to an idea. If you plan your speech so as not to create any gaps in thought, you will help your listeners to have an open mind. If you hit your audience with facts or judgments that contradict their way of thinking, they will shut down their ability to hear. Organize your presentation to allow the audience opportunity to fill in the gaps and stay open to your ideas.

### Cause and Effect

A speech organized by cause and effect presents a particular scenario, states what happened or may happen, and predicts a result. For example, if a community votes down a school bond issue, the effect may be crowded schools, fewer teachers, and fewer courses next year. If the government outlaws the use of radar detectors by truck drivers, then the effect might be safer highways, but slower delivery and higher prices for goods.

### Other Organization Options

In addition to the preceding methods of organizing your speech, you can also guide your audience from the known to the unknown, or from the easy to the difficult. These approaches work particularly well in a training situation. Suppose you are instructing others how to use a new software program. You could start with concepts that are already familiar to the group, building on them as a bridge to the unfamiliar.

## TYPES OF ORGANIZATION FOR PERSUASIVE SPEECHES

The best way to persuade people to take action is to focus their attention on the single step you want them to take when they leave. Although you can present other steps, more people will take action if you suggest they take a single step that seems like a manageable bite. When you drive one point home forcefully, it will be remembered.

Earlier, I recommended that you pick one aspect of your delivery and concentrate on changing just that aspect when you practice speaking. The principle is much the same when making a persuasive speech. Trying to change your rate of speech, varying your pitch, increasing your volume, and adding hand gestures all at once will lead to frustration rather than success.

If the purpose of your speech is to persuade your audience, the following organizational schemes are best:

- Motivated sequence.
- Problem to solution.
- Reflective order.
- Proposition to proof.

## Motivated Sequence

A speech organized by motivated sequence grabs the audience's attention, expresses a need and how that need can be satisfied, creates a vision of how circumstances will be different when that need is met, and then appeals to the audience's need to take action.

Television advertising in the longer format of "infomercials"— 30-minute programs that sell a single product—use this method of speaking. The "host" or speaker uses testimonials by people who have used the product or displays dramatic before-and-after photographs. The appeal to action is usually to send money or to order the product by charging it to a credit card. Actually, most commercials and sales presentations follow this same pattern.

## Problem to Solution

A speech organized this way states a problem in the introduction and persuades the audience to recognize a need for change. The body of the speech then presents a solution. The key to effectiveness with this approach is emphasizing and fully proving that the problem does exist and is significant, before moving on to the solution.

Use this type of organization when the audience does not realize that the problem exists or is of sufficient magnitude to require action. The main focus of your speech is convincing people of the need for change. An effective method is to point out the consequences of not addressing such problems—that they only get worse when ignored. For example, if you don't take your car in for a tune-up as soon as you suspect something is wrong, you may stall on the highway while on the way to an important meeting and hold up thousands of other drivers as well.

### Reflective Order

A persuasive speech that is ordered reflectively presents a known problem and then offers several alternatives. The speaker evaluates the alternatives in the body of the speech and selects the best. With reflective order, one also first proves a problem exists.

When addressing alternative solutions, effective speakers often present the positive points of each, then smash them with evidence to the contrary, and finally introduce the best alternative supporting it with ample evidence. Additionally, each alternative can be weighed against criteria you've established, with your desired alternative showing up as strongest.

For example, if you are speaking to a group of retail managers whose stores have lost market share in the past few months, you would start by giving that information.

> Our competitor has taken 22 percent of our market share since March! (Realistically, all in your audience already recognize that the problem exists.)

Then, you present two or more alternative solutions to the problem; methods the managers can use to regain customers. Any more than four solutions is counterproductive. You demonstrate throughout your speech that all the solutions you suggest have merit, but be sure to let the audience know the one that you want them to act on is the strongest alternative.

### Proposition to Proof

In a speech ordered in this manner, the introduction presents a proposition; the body of your speech then proves it. You conclude with an appeal to accept or act on your proposition.

When selecting any of these methods for either an informative or a persuasive speech, be sure to think of your audience. How knowledgeable are they about the topic? What is their attitude concerning the topic and you?

## USING INTERNAL SUMMARIES

Internal summaries are the glue of your speech. They maintain the flow of information, make connections between different points, and help your audience remember what they have heard.

An internal summary is a phrase such as:

> Now that we have talked about the advantages of Product A, Product B, and Product C, we will move on to Product D.

> I know you remember that earthquakes present a special hazard to schools because of the large numbers of children involved; now we'll talk about legislation that has been written to address this problem.

> As we've discussed, drug use in the work place costs a company in terms of increased sick days and absenteeism. It also has a dramatic affect on productivity . . .

You use internal summaries as transitions each time you switch from one of your main points to another. In fact, you can use an internal summary for just one point, if it is complex.

Just as your organization provides audience members with a road map, your internal summaries are signposts along the way. They let the audience know where they have been and where they are going.

# 13

# SUPPORTING MATERIALS

*I always think a great
orator convinces us not by
force of reasoning, but
because he is visibly
enjoying his beliefs, which
he wants us to accept.*
                —*J. B. Yeats*

Using data effectively in a speech will not ensure that you can sell a bad idea. Such information, however, can raise the likelihood that your listeners will accept ideas of merit.

You can begin collecting data as soon as you have selected your topic and limited it to your specific purpose. Brainstorm by asking yourself: What do I already know about the subject? What are the main points about this subject, and where are the holes in the information? You will want to fill in these gaps with additional research. I use post-it notes with all my brainstorming so that I can move my ideas around as I develop them.

Whenever you collect data, ensure that it is current and accurate, as well as relevant and acceptable to your listeners. Collecting materials that support the points in your speech probably will take the most time of all your efforts; once you have gathered your data, your preparation time will be 80 percent complete.

# HOW DATA CAN BE USED

## Substantiate Your Viewpoint

Facts and statistics can offer evidence about your viewpoint to persuade a skeptical audience. For example, if you are speaking about a new cancer treatment that merits more research dollars, then any evidence you can give to show increased survival rate or rate of cure because of the treatment will support your fund-raising efforts.

If you want an audience to take action, use statistics that illustrate what has happened in the past to people who took the same action. Suppose you're trying to convince a group that eating vegetables is healthy. A good approach might be to show that higher percentages of people who eat vegetables live longer with less heart disease than people who do not.

## Clarify a Point

Examples and stories can make a point clearer. If you want your audience to understand that current nutritional labeling on food packages is misleading, then you could show that a box of "Brand X Lite Cocoa" is just as expensive and high in calories as a box of regular "Brand X Cocoa."

The only difference in the two boxes—and you can open both packages and pour the suggested serving sizes into see-through measuring cups as you speak—is that the "Brand X Lite Cocoa" is referring to smaller servings than regular "Brand X Cocoa."

Demonstrations allow an audience to see as well as hear your point. As cited previously, people retain almost twice as much information if they see and hear about it than if they hear about it alone. Anything you can do to help the audience remember your point will make your presentation much more powerful. (We'll cover visual aids in Chapter 23.)

### *Make a Point Interesting*

Radon is not a subject that people naturally want to hear about. Since you can't see it, the way you might see crumbling asbestos insulation, testing for radon and arranging to lessen its effects is just another worry and expense on the average homeowner's list of things to do. Color slides used as visual aids would tend not to work.Data, however, can make a subject like radon more interesting by helping you put a more human face on the subject. How many people does it affect? With what consequences? How many people have improved the quality of their lives by testing for and taking care of a radon problem?

### *Involve Your Audience*

You can also use data to involve your audience by making them an extension of your research. For example, if you are speaking to an audience about the real estate market, you could ask them, "how many of you sold a home within the past two years? How many of you got the price that you originally asked for it?" After seeing a show of hands, you could then quote local and national statistics on the subject.

Questions like that get the audience alert, thoughtful, involved, and observant. People are basically self-serving. We all are. Being able to tie data to the experiences of people in the audience will make the subject come alive.

Audience involvement also helps overcome a problem created by sitting passively. If people sit for too long, their brains start to operate in a passive mode, and creative thought diminishes. Asking questions of the audience can break them out of the passive mode and get them thinking again. They will appreciate it.

### *Make the Point Memorable*

A presentation on AIDS would not be complete without a mention of Ryan White, the teenager who died of AIDS after spending the last few years of his life speaking out and educating the country about his disease.

Likewise a speech about homelessness seems unfinished without a discussion of the contributions of the late Mitch Snyder and the Center for Creative Non-Violence. Such examples can make your point memorable for your audience because they make an emotional connection.

## TYPES OF DATA

Your goal in collecting data is to enhance your main points with secondary information that is as colorful as possible. Tell stories, paint pictures, and use simple language so that your audience is listening to you and not scrambling to understand scientific words and jargon.

Define words, compare and contrast ideas, quote the recognized experts in the field, and bring visual aids with you so you can show as much as you tell.

You can employ data several ways within your presentation, including:

- Examples.
- Stories.
- Quotations.
- Definitions.
- Comparison and contrast.
- Statistics.
- Audiovisual aids.

### Examples

Examples can clarify, add interest, or make memorable, but they do not validate. For validation, you need facts and figures. An example would be a remark like this one: "All the staff members are working hard. For example, Joan stayed late three nights in a row . . ."

### Stories

A story is an account of an event or incident. People like to hear about the experiences of others. If you use a story, however, don't ramble or stretch out the anecdote beyond its significance.

The audience *will* want to hear some of your stories. After all, you are the expert on the subject at hand. Share some of your stories, but take care not to tell so many that you forget the purpose of your presentation.

### Quotations

A quotation is a statement by someone who is usually authoritative or experienced in the subject. Essentially the value of a quotation depends largely on the source—the author must be reputed to be knowledgeable, objective, and honest.

For some reason, quotations can sound profound although a peer who said the same words might sound silly. Quotations can often get a lot across with just a few words or sentences.

Opening with a quote that is contrary to your point can be a real attention getter. "There are no real leaders in the world today . . . according to . . . but I don't agree" would quickly grab the attention of business presidents and senior managers.

### Definitions

A definition is a statement of the meaning of the word or idea. A definition can help prove a point but is usually presented to make a point more understandable. Its major value is to establish a common basis for views with the audience.

A friend sat through a class called *Nonstructural Earthquake Hazard Mitigation for Hospitals*. At the end of the first day of this two-day class, the teacher gave a quiz. Grading the quiz, she realized that only 5 out of the 30 people in the class understood the definition of "mitigation."

Rather than assume that people understand definitions, it is far better to check or just to give the definition so you are all using the same road map.

## Comparison and Contrast

A comparison presents similar characteristics, features, and qualities; a contrast presents differences. They help clarify the unknown by referring to the known. We all find it easier to learn about something when we can relate it to something we already know. That's how we learned most of what we know now, by using our available knowledge as building blocks for future knowledge.

## Statistics

A statistic is a numerical fact or figure. You can increase the effectiveness of statistics by comparing the figure with some other fact known to the audience or easily comprehended by the audience.

For instance, If you were speaking on the total land area of all the islands that make up Japan, you could compare it to the size of California—it's roughly the same size—and any U.S. audience would understand immediately. Since you want people to get the major point, and not be bothered by insignificant details, round off your numbers.

## Audiovisual Aids

An audiovisual aid can be a recording, chart, diagram, model, computer aid, interactive presentation aid, slide, videotape, and so on. Audiovisuals allow you to present your case through an additional communication channel with your audience.

# 14

# THE CONCLUSION

*They may forget what you said—but they will never forget how you made them feel.*
—Carl W. Buehner

You've almost reached the end. You've made it through the planning, preparation, practice, and now almost through the presentation. I've seen speakers get to this point, breathe a sigh of relief, and blow it! Having a strong conclusion is vital.

In this chapter, we'll discuss how you can leave the audience with a favorable impression and an effective conclusion. As stated, your conclusion constitutes about 5 to 10 percent of your speech; its style should be consistent with the rest of your presentation.

The goal of your conclusion is multifold:

- To emphasize the purpose or key points of your speech. For example, if you're selling a product, you want to reiterate and accentuate its benefits and features, and remind the audience how the product will specifically help them. If you're discussing how to buy fine diamonds, as part of your conclusion emphasize the importance of the 4Cs—clarity, color, cut, and carats—in making an intelligent purchasing decision.

- To provide a climax to your talk. One of my favorite climaxes when talking about the value of practicing presentations is, "More people have talked their way up the ladder of success than have gotten there by any other way. You, too, can start climbing today."

- To leave the audience remembering your speech. The conclusion of John F. Kennedy's Inaugural Address serves as a good example, "Ask not what your country can do for you, ask what you can do for your country."

- To call them to action, if your purpose is to persuade your audience. The United Negro College Fund's ad, "A mind is a terrible thing to waste," has been very effective in persuading people to make donations.

# THE REVIEW

Your conclusion is best presented in two parts: a review of your subject, and a memorable statement. The two parts are joined by a transition statement. Let's tackle the review first.

### Review or Summarize Your Purpose

In just a few words, present a brief, an abstract, or an abridgement of the subject or the purpose of your speech. This can be pulled from the preview in your introduction. Summarizing the purpose usually reemphasizes the connection that your presentation has with the audience's needs or wants. You're answering, once more, the question they are asking, "What's in it for me?"

If you're speaking about wearing seat belts, a good summary statement would be:

> Given the evidence, are you willing to risk your life or health by not wearing seat belts? [completed by the memorable closing statement] Let's resolve today, that everyone in this room adopt using seat belts as a lifetime habit.

If you're speaking on donating to a particular charity, this summary would work:

If we all pull together and contribute as much as we can, we will be able to make this year's campaign the best ever. I am sure I can count on all of you to make this happen.

### *Repeat Your Main Points*

Following your brief abstract, repeat or rephrase the three to five main points you presented in the body of your speech. This can be done in one long, well-constructed sentence, or at most, one sentence for each point. If you have to use more than two sentences for any point, chances are the points were not sufficiently clear to begin with. Here's an example of a one-sentence repeat of the main points:

> As I've highlighted, XYZ corporation can meet your requirements for price reductions, flexibility in delivery dates, and quality standards in production.

### *Use a Transition Phrase*

After you've reviewed your speech, have a transition phrase handy to lead into your memorable statement. Transitions are not difficult; we use them all the time. They are vital to prevent gaps between you and your listeners. You use the transition between your review and your memorable statement for two reasons:

- It is all too easy to stop talking after you finish your main points. Having a transition phrase prepared will help you fight the natural urge to end prematurely.
- It prepares the audience for more.

Though you're working from an outline, write out verbatim the transition phrase you'll use. That way you will be able to make a smooth bridge to the final part of your speech. Here are some examples:

. . . and so I ask you . . .

. . . which leads me to the say . . .

. . . and so my fellow Americans . . .

. . . and if there's one thing that bears repeating . . .

## THE MEMORABLE STATEMENT

There are four basic options in presenting a final, memorable statement:

- Using a new grabber in contrast to your opening grabber.
- Returning to the opening grabber.
- Looking to the future.
- Calling for action.

### Using a New "Grabber"

You can select a new and different memorable statement with the same techniques you used to grab the attention of your audience in the introduction of your speech: Ask a question, state an unusual fact, give an illustration, example, or story, or present a quotation.

For example if your opening grabber was "How would you like to make a difference in the war on drugs in your community?" your closing grabber could be "If you follow these guidelines, you can achieve the same outstanding results achieved in XYZ community."

Here's a second example. If your opening grabber was "How many of you have experienced symptoms of stage fright when giving a speech?" the close could be "Remember, your goal is not to get rid of the butterflies, but to have them fly in formation."

### Returning to the Opening Grabber

A particularly effective way to close is to present the same story, quotation, or other device that you used as your introduction, but with a different ending, or an additional line, or another insight or explanation. For example:

> So, while you can't take it with you, at least you can be sure your estate will be in safekeeping for your heirs.

### *Looking to the Future*

Pointing to the future extends to your audience the invitation to consider, explore, and think further about your subject:

> By providing our services to you, we'll be building a partnership between our companies that will enable both to be more profitable in the next decade.

### *Calling for Action*

A call to action is suitable when the purpose of your speech is to persuade the audience. You have established a need or problem, and you have presented what is necessary to satisfy the need or solve the problem in the body of your speech. It follows logically that in the conclusion you would call your audience to action. For example:

> Board members, with the benefits we presented, I urge you to vote to accept our proposal today, so we can initiate the program by February.

## A SELF TEST

To pretest your conclusion, ask yourself these questions:

- Does my conclusion put the audience where I want them at the end of my speech?
- Does my conclusion finish my presentation by leaving my audience sure of what I want them to know, feel, or do?

If you feel confident in the answers to these two questions, then you'll have a strong conclusion.

## SOME DO'S AND DON'TS FOR CONCLUSIONS

*Don'ts*

1. Don't apologize.

2. Don't stretch it out.

3. Don't merely stop.

4. Don't introduce new points.

5. Don't pack up early.

6. Don't continue to speak as you leave the lectern.

*Do's*

1. Do work on your conclusion carefully.

2. Do end with strength.

3. Do get to the point and summarize.

4. Do bring your speech to a smooth ending.

5. Do signal your audience that you are concluding.

# 15

## ANSWERING QUESTIONS

*There are no dumb answers, only smart questions.*
                    *—Aristotle*

*The only dumb question is the one not asked.*
                    *—Anonymous*

Often speakers come to the end of their speeches wanting to get away from the podium as quickly as possible. They do not want to take any questions; instead, they just want to sit down and meld in with everyone else. *Do not* do that. Your presentation does not end with your conclusion. If you end hastily, you're missing an opportunity to advance your ideas further and to clarify your comments in a *question-and-answer* session.

## ENCOURAGING QUESTIONS FROM YOUR AUDIENCE

Once you have concluded your speech, you may see people raising their hands to ask questions. Sometimes there are no hands. Don't assume that your speech was so clear that everyone understood it. If people are not asking questions, it means one of several things:

1. They are bored.
2. They are confused.
3. They are afraid they will look stupid by asking questions in front of others.
4. They are turned off by your presentation.
5. They want to leave.

As the speaker, you want to encourage questions from your audience. You can do this nonverbally by stepping out from behind the podium, if possible, and demonstrating an open body language. Then people will feel that you are approachable.

You can encourage questions verbally by asking, "Do you have any questions?" or "What questions do you have?" which are phrased as though you really want questions. Then pause and wait for questions. If you pose the question and then move on to your farewell, or begin packing away your visual aids, then the audience will think you do not really have time to take questions.

It makes good sense to come prepared with your own questions, and if there are still no questions from the audience, you can say, "A question I'm usually asked is . . . ," or "when I first studied this subject I wondered about . . ."

## WHEN TO TAKE QUESTIONS

Your audience will be able to formulate questions if you give them an early warning. At the same time that you preview your subject in the introduction to your speech, tell them when they can ask questions.

### Handling Questions during Your Presentation

There are two times when it makes sense to handle questions during a presentation:

- If you are giving a training or sales presentation, you may want your audience to ask questions at any time. You want to be careful, however, because you can get off onto tangents easily, or jump too far ahead, and lose the attention of your listeners.

- Take questions from your audience at breaking points at the end of each section. Tell people to hold their questions until these breaks.

You can, of course, take questions from your audience at the end of your speech. Ask people to hold their questions until the end. Always communicate openly with people who have questions; don't rebuff them. If someone asks a question at an inappropriate time, explain that you want to answer the question, but that you're in a building process; then ask the person to write the question down and you will discuss it at the end of the section or the end of the speech. As long as you communicate effectively with people, they will accept your guidelines.

### The Value in Delaying

By delaying questions to the end of a section or speech, you give your audience a chance to think about and form their questions. However, use your own judgment. If your subject is a highly technical one, you may want to answer questions as they are posed to help the audience understand your topic.

Many in your audiences will be eager to ask questions. If they seem hesitant, however, it is your duty to encourage them to interact.

## RESPONDING TO DIFFERENT TYPES OF QUESTIONS

There are three reasons people ask questions:

1. They want to get information.
2. They want to expand on their own ideas.
3. They want to trap you in a 'gotcha' question.

You do not have to know everything, but it is important to carry yourself well, keep the session moving along, and give the impression that if you do not know an answer, you are certainly going to pursue it and be prepared the next time that question comes up.

## When You Know the Answer

First, don't overcompliment the questioner, or provide a value judgment by saying, "That's a good question." When you compliment one questioner and not another, you are implying that the second question is not as good as the first. The question asked may be developmental; we wouldn't want to pass judgment on someone's developmental process.

The best way to respond when you know the answer is first to rephrase the question. You don't have to do it all the time, but it is a good way of making sure both that you understand the question and that everyone else heard it.

It took me several years to feel comfortable rephrasing people's questions and to remember to do it, so do not feel badly if it does not come naturally to you. It is a listening skill we can all benefit from developing and using in daily conversations.

Rephrasing the question also buys you more time to formulate your answer in the best possible way. Look at the question-and-answer session during any presidential news conference and you will see how the President rephrases questions and gathers his thoughts all the while. It gives you time to ask yourself, "What is the motivation behind that question?"

After answering, avoid the tendency to come back and ask, "Did I answer your question?" If the person says no, then you look stupid. If she thinks no, but answers yes so she does not look stupid, then she still has not received an answer to her question. It is a weak response in a lose–lose situation.

A better way to make sure you answered the question is to ask the same person, "What other questions do you have?" Then neither of you looks stupid, and the door is open for further questions.

## *When You Don't Know the Answer*

If you don't know the answer to a question, *do not lie.* You are going to get caught, and it isn't worth it. When preparing your speech, anticipate tough spots by asking yourself, "What is the toughest question I could be asked on this subject?" Find the answers and be prepared. However, if you do get a question you can't answer, the best response is to say, "I'm sorry, I don't have that information." Then you have several options.

1. If it is a specific question, answer it generally, and then tell the person that you need to get more facts together. If you promise to get back to the person later, then do it. You can have your questioners write their questions on the back of a business card, which will serve as a reminder to you.

2. If you cannot get back with the correct answer, then give the person a source for obtaining the information.

3. You can throw the question back and ask, "I don't know, what do you think?"

4. Keep moving. Don't linger if you do not know an answer. Two things will never happen no matter how long you wait: You'll never know the answer; and the questioner will never say, "It's OK, I really did not want an answer."

## *When You Meet Up with a "Stage Hog"*

A stage hog is someone who asks one question after another monopolizing the question-and-answer session. When someone is asking a series of legitimate questions that involve the whole group, then it's OK to keep the dialogue going.

Often, the stage hog is someone not in power who just wants to hear his own voice. You need to get rid of him fast. If you don't, the situation will only get worse. The first time, answer his question. Initially, the audience will be on your side if you do not attack him back. However, if you let him continue, the audience will turn on you.

When the red flag goes up that your questioner is a stage hog, you can say, "It sounds like you have a lot of good questions and you need some time, but right now I want to make sure that everyone has an opportunity to ask questions. If you write yours down now and meet me after the presentation, I'll be glad to answer them. Now, what questions do the rest of you have?"

As you say this, turn your body away from the stage hog. You don't want to minimize him, but you can't let him take control. The rest of the group will be thankful you shut him up.

If the stage hog continues to raise his hand with questions, tell him each time to write his question down and add that you will discuss it with him later. After the presentation, be available to meet with him. If he's just out to cause problems, he won't show up.

If you know someone is a stage hog before your presentation, you could feed his ego by meeting with him in advance and incorporating some of his ideas into your speech—a strategy that helps get him on your side from the beginning. Also, you could let your audience know in advance that you are limiting each person to one question each.

A technique I've used with people who run long in their comments without coming to a question is to hook subtly onto their idea and finish the thought for them. By bringing their comments to a close, you can quickly move on, announcing to the rest of the audience that "there is time for one more question on this topic."

### When There Is an Expert in the Audience

If someone poses a question, and you know there is a person in the audience who can answer the question better than you, then call on that expert. It is a courtesy, however, to say the expert's name aloud to get her attention, and then rephrase the question, just in case she was not paying attention.

Once the expert is talking, all the attention and control of the situation has left you and is now in the hands of the expert. It is up to you to thank the expert and take control back by turning the attention to the next question. The longer you let the attention go to the stage hog or the expert, the harder it is to bring it back.

If you choose to give up control (sometimes politically astute) then move off to the side or sit down. When you want to regain control, move back to the spot from which you were speaking. The audience will follow your movement.

## HANDLING QUESTIONS FROM A HOSTILE AUDIENCE

You want always to know what your audience thinks and feels so that you can be prepared with answers to their questions. Presumably you also have structured your presentation so as not to offend your audience and to keep communication open.

If you are anticipating hostile questions, set up guidelines ahead of time. For example, you could say, "We have three minutes for questions." Be aware of your body language and do not allow yourself to slip into the combative stance by crossing your arms, backing off, or getting into a locked stare with any one person in the audience.

Don't engage in a battle of hostile questions. You cannot win! If someone asks you a sensitive question and you go on the defensive, then they will hit you with other questions, and you will defend again while the battle escalates.

It takes two people to create hostility, and it is up to you, as the one in control, not to let this happen. Clench your teeth, bite your tongue, or take a breath to maintain control.

### You Are the Messenger, Not the Message

If you are speaking about budget cutbacks to company supervisors, there is bound to be hostility, but you don't have to take the heat for upper management's decision. Acknowledge up front that it is an abhorrent situation. Use humor to defuse some of the anger. Take time to understand your audience's point of view.

If someone asks a question that you do not like, you could throw it back to the person. Ask, "What is your point?" or say, "That is one way of looking at it."

A better approach is to follow a simple 4-step formula to handle people who are attacking you:

1. Let the person vent out his anger by expressing what he feels. Dig your feet in, take a breath, but do not interrupt no matter how his comments might enflame you. Let him have his say and get the negative energy out.

2. Paraphrase the person's statement, by saying something like, "I can see that your concerns seem to be centered on . . ." Once you listen, show the person respect, and show the person that you understand how he feels, you have been able to take the wind out of his sails. You may not agree with what he said, but you allowed him to say it.

3. Ask the person a question, such as "Did this problem always exist?" Shrink the disagreement down to something tangible and specific. Ask him to get information.

4. Either refute the person's view or problem solve. In some cases you do not refute, for example, if you are in customer service and you are speaking to an audience of your customers.

If only one person is hostile, you can always ask the rest of the group how they feel. Giving them a chance to talk on the subject will put them on your side.

If you do your homework and get a good reading on your audience and where they are coming from in advance, you won't have a problem with hostility.

## CONCLUDING THE SESSION

If you are out of time, or there are no more questions, it is time to end your presentation. Never just say "thank you" and leave. You need *another* conclusion at the end of the question-and-answer session. Return to your central theme, revert to your closing statement, or talk about what will happen next. To wrapup your presentation, you might say:

All right, now it is time for all of you to take this information and start using it yourself to have a very successful career. Thank you.

Keep your question-and-answer session moving along by listening to your audience's comments and understanding what they are saying. Use the session as an opportunity to advance and clarify your ideas, and you will be able to end it with a strong finish.

---

**CHECKLIST: MAKING THE MOST OF YOUR QUESTION-AND-ANSWER SESSIONS**

☐ Encourage questions with positive phrasing and body language.

☐ Let the audience know early when you will answer questions.

☐ Listen carefully and rephrase a question before you answer.

☐ When repeating, look at the questioner; when answering, look at the entire audience.

☐ If you don't know an answer, don't lie.

☐ Don't let the "stage hog" take control.

☐ Call on experts in the audience, but take back attention.

☐ If you anticipate hostile questions, set a time limit.

☐ Let the questioner vent anger, then refute or problem solve.

☐ Respect the questioner; don't be defensive.

☐ Answer briefly.

☐ Always be positive.

☐ End the question-and-answer session with a closing statement.

# COMMUNICATING ON PURPOSE

## WHAT'S IN IT FOR YOU

In Chapter 16, you will glean the characteristics of an informative presentation and the keys to informative speaking. If you follow the planning sheet, you'll include all the information you need to give an informative presentation.

To persuade an audience, you have to have opened the audiences' mind to your subject. You'll understand the dynamics of persuasion in Chapter 17. The methods of persuasive proof and proper organization of your material will become clear to you in this section.

If you make sales presentations, don't skip Chapter 18. You'll learn how to demonstrate need to your customers and offer a solution to that need. The chapter also provides tips to help you make the sale.

We are all faced with the need to give impromptu presentations daily. If you find yourself speaking "off the cuff" often, Chapter 19 will be of benefit. You'll learn how to take advantage of the opportunity to deliver an impromptu speech.

To determine your audience's needs, you'll have to listen. Part Four would not be complete without tips for listening. Chapter 20 is a brief review of the most effective listening advice to help you really hear what's being said.

# 16

# INFORMATIVE SPEAKING

*As we become proficient in our area of specialization or assume positions of increased responsibility, we shall be called on more and more to convey to others information we have acquired.*
*— Roger P. Wilcox*

An informative speech relays new information. You want to hold the audience's interest, and you want them to retain the information that you give them.

The preceding quote, by Roger P. Wilcox of the General Motors Institute, describes the essence of informative speaking. As a subject matter expert you are in the position to give information to others, and you want to give it as effectively as possible.

## FOUR CHARACTERISTICS OF AN INFORMATIVE SPEECH

To be effective, your informative speech needs to have four characteristics:

127

1. *An Informative Speech Contains New and Useful Information for Its Audience.* If a speech to inform contains no information that is new *to the audience,* it does not perform the function of informing at all. If your speech is about the difficulties women have balancing work, motherhood, and the home, then chances are you will be revealing no new information on this time-worn subject.

   If you choose to speak on the topic of businesses that are creating day-care centers at the workplace or companies that offer paternity leave for men, then you may have a fresher slant on the subject, and you can research and assemble new information to offer your audience. The speech to inform *instructs,* not merely *helps* an audience pass the time pleasantly.

2. *An Informative Speech Helps the Audience Understand and Retain Information.* An informative speech is organized in a systematic way that helps people take the information in, assimilate it, and retain it. New and useful information can best be learned when it has a meaningful pattern. A well-organized speech helps with any instruction. For example, in describing how to ensure that a meeting is effective, you could inform your audience of the responsibilities of a leader *before, during,* and *after* the meeting.

3. *An Informative Speech Presents Information in an Appealing Manner.* Because the information in your speech is important to the audience and is well organized does not mean that your informative speech will be received favorably. Whereas a dry textbook on astronomy will give the basic facts about outer space, a speaker like Carl Sagan can make us feel as if we are traveling in space ourselves, here on earth.

   Sagan speaks passionately because he loves his subject. He brings the science of outer space to an everyday level, so that we can envision the principles of physics displayed in the environment around us, be it in the food we eat or in the experience of riding a bicycle down a winding street. Your speech needs to be just as vivid, delivered to maximize learning and make your subject as appealing as possible. Enjoyment increases learning.

4. *It Motivates the Audience to Learn the Information.* People learn best when they are motivated to do so. Your goal is to make your audience want to learn. During your introduction, point out the importance of your information to the audience and then continually relate your subject matter to their needs, wants, and desires throughout the speech.

For example, we all need to know how to protect ourselves and what steps to take in an emergency, such as a flood or earthquake. Trying to teach others emergency preparedness, however, when the sun is shining and there hasn't been a flood or earthquake in years is difficult. You can motivate such audiences by highlighting the plight of people in supposedly "safe" areas who had to deal with natural disasters, or by tying in emergency preparedness with general safety.

## THREE KEYS WHEN YOU SPEAK TO INFORM

People learn better when the speaker gives *small amounts* of information, *repeats it often*, and relates it to *principles*:

1. *Introduce Small Amounts.* People need time to receive, digest, and reflect on the information you are presenting. Narrow your topic and select pertinent points to present to your audience. For example, if you are speaking to retired persons about health benefits offered through Medicare, then you need to refine your topic to a certain aspect of Medicare, such as who is eligible, how to apply for benefits, or the effect of recent legislation on Medicare.

2. *Repeat Often.* Repeat your salient points several times during your speech, including different words, pictures, and stories. People remember information when they hear it reiterated. Previewing what you're going to tell your audience, providing periodic internal summaries, and reviewing what you've

told them all help emphasize your message in a palatable manner.

3. *Stress the Principle.* General principles and major concepts are better comprehended and retained than details or specifics. The clearer the general principle, the better it will be retained. Limit your topic to only a few general principles, however. If you must present a large number of details, make printed copies of the information and distribute them. Do not overload your audience or they will tune out.

The following sample planning sheet will help you organize an informative presentation.

Finally, if you are preparing to give an informative speech, remember that such a speech doesn't contain specific and concrete details as an end in themselves, but as a means for explaining, exemplifying, and amplifying the important ideas.

## INFORMATIVE SPEECH PLANNING SHEET

Specific purpose of this speech _____

_____

Method of organization _____

_____

The audience _____

_____

*Introduction*

1. Grabber Statement

2. WIIFT

3. Source Credibility

4. Preview Statement

*Body*

1.

Supporting Material

2.

3.

Transitions

4.

*Conclusion*

1. Review

2. Memorable Statement

# 17

## *PERSUASIVE SPEAKING*

*He who seizes the right
moment is the right man.*
*—Goethe*

The Greek philosopher Aristotle is known as the father of public speaking. Aristotle believed that all speaking is persuasion. Quintillian, another rhetorician, defined a good speaker as "a good man [person] speaking well." Some would say that Adolph Hitler was one of the most outstanding speakers of the twentieth century—Quintillian would passionately disagree. Hitler was effective in meeting his own purpose, but he wasn't a good person by most people's moral standards.

We would certainly all agree that there is enormous power in persuasive speaking. This is obvious in TV commercials, mob psychology, and sales technology. If you have ever impulsively bought something after hearing a sales pitch, arrived home, and thought, "Now, why did I buy that?" then you have felt the power of persuasive speaking.

That's what we'll explore in this chapter—how you can persuade people to share your point of view. I hope that you want to be a good person of strong personal character speaking well, as you persuade people to develop themselves.

Aristotle used three methods of "proof" in persuasive speaking that are just as valid today as when he used them.

## THREE METHODS OF PERSUASIVE PROOF

### Logos

Translated from Greek, *logos*, which means "logic," is your factual presentation of evidence. Logos uses reason supported by research data. Logos includes statistics, documentation, testimony, supporting evidence, and hard facts. This type of information is often slanted because presenters can choose the facts to support one point of view and exclude the others. While an informative speech can stand on logic alone, a persuasive speech needs the other two methods of proof to succeed.

### Pathos

The second method of persuasive proof is *pathos*, which refers to feeling and emotion. Pathos is the emotional part of our being, making us feel sympathetic or empathetic to someone. Use this method to motivate your audience. Appeal to their basic social, biological, and psychological needs, wants, and desires.

It is important to understand that people make decisions with a combination of logos and pathos, though our society and our culture believe that we make valuable decisions solely on the basis of intellect (logos).

Abraham Maslow's research demonstrates that we have a hierarchy of needs to be satisfied, which first includes existence needs: food, water, and shelter. Once we have met these needs, we become aware of our relationship needs: a sense of belonging, family, status, and ego. When these needs have been met, we then experience fulfillment needs: spirituality, self-actualization, and the making of a contribution to society. We are motivated by our own needs, not someone else's. When we buy a product or service, we are doing so because we hope to fulfill our most dominant needs. Understanding need fulfillment is vital to persuasion.

Fund-raising speeches are probably the epitome of persuasion. I've trained people who raise funds for national charities in powerful presentation skills. Asking people to give money without expecting anything concrete in return requires the use of pathos. The outcome of your message is for your audience to feel good and feed their ego by donating, and to feel guilty if they *don't* help others by giving money.

While the evidence, or logos, weighs heavily in making a decision, do not underestimate the power of pathos, which is best used in moderation. If a persuasive speaker hits you with excessive pathos, the emotion will fade when you walk away, and unless the facts are there, you won't return to buy.

Ultimately when you return to your home or work environment, your opinions will shift. That's why many hard-sell salespeople will try to get you to sign on the dotted line immediately after their sales pitch.

Conversely, if a persuasive speaker concentrates on logos and adds a little pathos, the chances of your buying into a belief or product is stronger. By knowing your audience and their "hot buttons," you can address their specific emotional needs.

### Ethos

*Ethos* means "ethics" or "standards." In persuasive speaking, ethos relates to influencing your audience through your credibility as a speaker. Ethos is how you carry yourself, what kind of education and background you present, or your known position with the company or on a topic.

Ethos has more to do with how people perceive you than with who you really are. For example, many people will vote for a Democratic candidate strictly because of the party affiliation and not because of who the candidate is, or what he or she really thinks. We listen selectively based on our perceptions of people. As you speak, your audience is judging and evaluating you.

In successful persuasion, all three methods—logos, pathos, and ethos—are mixed in varying degrees, depending on the speaker's analysis of the audience, or his or her character and style.

# A FOUR-COLUMN APPROACH TO YOUR PERSUASIVE SPEECH

When you are ready to prepare your persuasive speech, divide a sheet of paper into four columns, as shown in the following chart.

The following subsections describe the four columns of the chart.

| PERSUASIVE SPEAKING | | | |
|---|---|---|---|
| *Purpose* | *Audience* | *Data* | *Organization* |
| Motivate | Favorable | Current | Proposition to proof |
| Convince | Uninformed | Accurate | Problem to solution |
| Call to action | Apathetic | Useful | Reflective |
|  | Hostile | Relevant | Motivated sequence |
|  | Mixed | Acceptable |  |

## The Purpose Column

In the first column, decide which of three levels of persuasion to use with your audience:

1. **Motivate.** The first level is to motivate your audience. You don't want to change their opinion or alter their beliefs, but you do want to get them excited about something, full of energy and feeling good. A coach's locker room pep talk before a big game or a candidate's address at a political rally invokes feelings of motivation. The keynote speech at an annual convention, or a church sermon is motivational in nature.

2. **Convince Your Audience.** The next level of persuasion is to convince an audience to shift opinion from their point of view to yours. If they have no point of view, then you want to be the first to influence them. You don't necessarily want

them to do anything; you simply want them to believe as you do.

3. **Call Your Audience to Action.** The most difficult level of persuasion is to actuate or call your audience to action. Here you want them to accept your proposal, make a phone call, follow new company procedures, write their senator, donate money, give you a raise or whatever.

Many persuasive speeches attempt actuation but don't succeed. Public service announcements on television tell us to quit smoking, but they may not be as successful at calling us to action as, say, commercials that sell stop-smoking gimmicks such as timers or special filters. We know it's wise to eat properly, but how many people actually do it daily? That's the difference between what you believe and what you do.

In this first column, make your purpose clear. What do you want your audience to do when your speech is over? Be energized? Believe? Take action? Your purpose is your bottom line. Write it down to use as a benchmark. Ask yourself after your presentation: Did I ask for what I wanted? Did I get it? If not, what do I need to do differently next time?

## The Audience Column

Now we need to briefly review material covered in Chapter 8, "Knowing your Audience." Before you can persuade your audience to do what you want, you have to know who they are. In this second column, determine what kind of audience attitudes you face—*favorable, uninformed, apathetic, hostile,* or *mixed*—because you need to understand your audience to plan a strategy and to be effective presenting to them.

Changing an audience's attitude can be a difficult task. If their attitudes and beliefs are fixed, you might settle for a chance to speak your piece and hope you'll get a fair hearing.

Realistically, you cannot expect to gain agreement with just one speech, no matter how convincing you are. If your listeners are open-minded, however, you may be able to swing some moderates among them to your banner.

- Favorable audiences already agree with you and want what you want (e.g., a conservative Republican speaking to conservative Republicans).

- Uninformed audiences are not opposed to what you say, they just don't know anything about it. You need to educate them. For example, if you want me to give money to El Salvador, first determine if I know where it is, the trouble it's facing, and how people are being affected.

- Apathetic audiences do not care and must be convinced that something will affect or benefit them before they will respond. For example, few people think or care about landfills—unless one is going to be located next door. To keep a landfill from being built in your neighborhood, you need to rally all the neighbors by convincing them that the landfill will affect their quality of life.

- Hostile audiences are not necessarily opposed to you, but you do have to find where their hostilities lie. For example, a woman goes in to talk to her boss because she wants a raise, and her boss is hostile. To win him over, she speaks eloquently about what a good job she's doing, but he already knows what a good worker she is. The issue isn't her performance, it's the budget. Unless she addresses the budget issue and understands what his hostility is about, her quest is vain.

- Mixed audiences are any combination of the other four audiences. The minute there are a few hostile people in a mixed audience, however, it tends to become hostile because those few people are going to surface issues that may set the others against you.

## The Data Column

Now that you have defined your purpose and pinpointed your audience, you are ready to collect data. Your third column reflects the sources you plan to tap.

As with the informative speech, your data should be current, accurate, useful, relevant, and acceptable. Audiences do not learn by interesting sidebars or tangents to your subject—make your facts straightforward, credible, and representative of a broad consensus of opinion.

For example, if I am going to take a pronuclear stand while speaking to a mixed or hostile audience and all my information is from one source—the Nuclear Regulatory Commission—is the audience going to think my source is credible? Not likely. There will be little opportunity for me to shift them unless I broaden my sources and use both logos and pathos.

### The Organization Column

After determining your purpose, analyzing the audience, and collecting accurate information, you then need to select the method of organization that will help you achieve your purpose. Options for the persuasive speech are proposition to proof, problem to solution, reflective, or motivated sequence.

*Proposition to Proof.* In the "proposition to proof" method, you state your proposition at the beginning of your speech so the audience knows what you want them to believe or do. Then you prove your proposition with 3 to 5 points of evidence and an emotional appeal. Finally, you review your evidence and give a memorable closing statement. It is a simple, straightforward method.

Your most crucial task is deciding whether this method of organization is right for the audience you are addressing. The objective of persuasive speaking is to keep the audience open-minded for as long as possible. If you hit them early with something that is going to offend them, and they cannot accept your point of view, they close down. To make people willing to change, present them new experiences and new information in a manner they can assimilate.

*Problem to Solution.* In the "problem to solution" method of organization, state the problem and then offer a solution from your point of view. Depending on the problem's complexity, you might have to spend 75 percent of your speech explaining the problem from your point of view. After all, how can your audience agree on a solution if they cannot agree that a problem exists and that it should be defined in the same terms that you would choose.

Spend time developing your definition of the problem with logos and pathos. Follow it with your solution; then present three to five points and supporting material, your review, and a memorable statement.

An example of a speech using this method of organization would be a speech about the energy crisis. While keeping the audience open-minded, I might spend time explaining the problem and the need for developing alternative energy sources. Then I would propose my solution, which is to continue developing nuclear power.

*Reflective.*   The preceding method would be too simplistic for a hostile audience. The "reflective" method of organization might work better: Consider that there are as many solutions to most problems as there are attitudes and ideas from your audience.

In the reflective method, start with a problem and prove it exists. Establish the criteria to accept a solution. Then define the solutions that you do not like; discuss the benefits of those solutions, then refute and smash them, proving that the negatives so far outweigh the positive that only your solution (from your viewpoint) will work.

People fail using this method when they present the positive and the negatives in a balanced fashion. You cannot persuade people without a dramatic tip of the scales. Give them no way to agree on anything except your solution.

Clearly dismiss other points of view one by one, as you prove their flaws. You may not be able to change others' views, but you can discredit them. By the time you finish, only one possibility appears to be desirable.

*Motivated Sequence.*   The fourth method of organization is a well-known sales technique called "motivated sequence." This is the only organizational method that takes your persuasive speech all the way to a call to action. If you want a call to action in the other three methods, you have to build it in yourself.

The motivated sequence makes the audience aware of a need for change, or creates that need. The speaker brings the audience to the brink of asking for help to change and then supplies the means for making that change.

For example, a television advertising salesperson might approach a client with a bleak picture of the current economy and facts about how other local businesses increased their sales through investing in advertising on television. Once the client is hooked, the salesperson whips out time slot schedules that provide maximum coverage for the client's budget.

One note: When you want to highlight the features of a product or service, don't just explain the features—tell what those features will do for your audience.

For example, if you are selling a car that has an 8-cylinder engine, explain that those 8 cylinders will provide more immediate speed than a regular engine, so that passing on two-lane roads is much safer. Bring up any disadvantages early on, refute them, and move on.

### Aid Your Converts

Suppose you are speaking to an audience, and you manage to convince one listener to take action. This person is not a decision maker and so has to convince her boss, who is hostile. You are doing your convert a disservice by not preparing her and arming her with the negative point of view.

If the buck does not stop with your audience, you need to know where it does stop so that you can adequately support your point of view—more than you need for your audience, but enough to satisfy the decision maker back on the job.

Knowing how to speak persuasively is crucial to the achievement of your career goals. When you can change other people's beliefs, reinforce their current attitudes, or convince them to take action that you want them to take, then you are a persuasive speaker.

## CHECKLIST: PLANNING YOUR PERSUASIVE SPEECH

☐ What are you trying to accomplish? What is your purpose in speaking?

☐ How does your audience feel toward your purpose and position?

☐ What emotional and psychological appeals will move these people?

☐ What logical reasoning will "reach" them?

☐ Are they willing to accept new ideas?

☐ Why does this audience want to listen to you?

# 18

# EFFECTIVE SALES PRESENTATIONS

*Salesmanship consists of*
*transferring a conviction*
*from a seller to a buyer.*
*—Arnold H. Glasgow*

Although a sales presentation is also a persuasive talk, there are enough differences to discuss them separately.

The first step in a successful sales presentation is to gain the attention of your audience, create goodwill, and establish your credibility. There are several possible approaches:

- Grabber openings such an *example, illustration,* or *story* with a point.
- Humorous *anecdote* that makes a point.
- *Quotations* from an easily recognized personality.
- *Striking statement.*
- *Rhetorical question* that gets the audience members thinking.
- *Personal greeting* or a *reference to the subject or occasion.*

## DEMONSTRATE A NEED

The next step is to identify and highlight a general problem and relate it to the needs of the audience. If your research before the presentation is thorough enough to understand their needs, you'll be better able to express them in terms of a problem that your product or service can solve.

Begin by stating the need, using a direct statement that describes an undesirable situation that could be improved or strengthened. I'll use the same example all the way through this discussion so you can see how the concepts work.

Suppose you are a Human Resources Manager and have met with a representative for a temporary labor services firm. You have discussed the temporary services offered and need to sell the idea of using their firm internally. You could begin by respectfully and tactfully saying to your audience, "There is a lack of professionally trained assistants in this company."

Next, you would illustrate the need by telling stories or giving examples, such as, "Last week, the company missed its deadline for the planned mass mailing because the labels were not printed."

Now that the audience is getting a feel for how bad the problem is, you develop the need further through additional examples, statistics, or testimonies that show more about the problem. "Over the past 12 months, deadlines for five marketing campaigns have been missed, and the turnover among the company's secretaries and administrative assistants is extremely high because they feel overburdened and undercompensated, yet there are no funds budgeted for hiring additional full-time employees."

By now, members of the audience will be able to visualize the need. Show how the problem affects the members of the audience and what it will do to them.

> Remember, we all think in terms of "what's in it for me?" Likewise with a problem; the need can be seen much more clearly if people see a personal and direct connection.

To return to our example, you might next say: "The delays in the marketing campaigns have resulted in a 10 percent drop in business this year. If this continues for another quarter, the company will be forced to lay off 25 employees."

## OFFERING A SOLUTION

Since the listeners now understand how the problem affects them and how the need impacts on them on the personal level, let them know that your service or product can solve the problem.

Explain the features of your product and show how the features will benefit the client. Give evidence by using examples, testimony, statistics, or telling a story. For our example, you could say, "ABC Company has skilled temporary secretarial help that can be used as much or little as you need to make sure all your marketing deadlines are met."

Next, overcome any objections the audience raises by answering them. Even if no one says anything, *begin discussing possible objections (and answers to them) that you identified before you started the sales presentation.*

By raising the objections yourself and then answering them, you have made it easy for the audience to share their concerns. Many will feel you have settled the need for them to raise objections and will appreciate your effort.

## VISUALIZATION AND ACTION

The purpose of this step is to intensify the desire of the client to move ahead with the proposed solution. Describe how things will be after your solution is adopted. Urge the client to take the action you propose. The objective is to bring the presentation to a close with a sense of completeness that prompts the audience to action.

To do so, first summarize the benefits to the client, directly request that the audience take action, and induce them with an offer of some additional benefit for taking the action you propose.

Then, review what has preceded, and invite definite action from the group.

To close, you might say, "Hiring temporary help from ABC Company will allow you to meet your marketing deadlines without the expense of hiring full-time help. All you have to do is call me, and I will have a professional at your door within four hours. If you call this week, we will give you eight hours of work free. Your deadlines will be met, your current secretaries and assistants will be relieved to have the extra help, and your budget won't suffer. I look forward to serving you starting immediately. Here is my telephone number."

## *GENERALIZATIONS ABOUT THE PERSUASION AND SELLING*

No matter how skillfully you prepare your sales presentation, your words alone will not carry the day. Other subtle factors influence whether you can persuade an audience to act. Attitude or behavior change is more likely when the speaker is perceived as believable.

The speaker who is viewed as being credible, having product knowledge, being enthusiastic, and having no secret agendas will be regarded as trustworthy.

A speaker who arouses anger or resentment will immediately be viewed as unfavorable. The client will also have a negative impression of the company represented by the person. When a speaker is viewed favorably, he reflects a positive image of the organization he represents.

If you are unknown to your listeners, you can raise credibility by decreasing the number of verbalized pauses in the presentation, being well organized, and using correct pronunciation and effective delivery.

Listeners tend to be favorable toward the speaker's message if they see themselves as having similar attitudes and goals. The persuasiveness of any message, even one attributed to a respected speaker, disappears over time. The impact can be reinstated by reminding the listeners of what you said.

The ability to empathize accurately with the client is a key to effective persuasion and communication. The speaker who is not attuned to his listener's needs is unlikely to succeed.

## GENERALIZATIONS ABOUT LISTENERS

Listeners selectively receive and interpret messages in terms of their existing knowledge, attitudes, and current needs. A listener is more receptive and retentive when the message is consistent with his knowledge, attitudes, and needs. Messages phrased in terms of the client's needs and interests are more successful. Speak their language, acronyms, and slang.

Features or recommendations are best phrased as benefits to the client. A feature describes a characteristic of the product, service, or recommendation of the speaker. A benefit can be viewed as a "what this means to you" statement. The effective salesperson persistently and explicitly relates features to the client's benefits.

Mental or verbal participation by the client improves the chance that he or she will be persuaded. This is why rhetorical questions, to the audience that cause them to visualize the situation you are discussing, are effective in persuasive speaking. Finally, the key to successful speaking is always to answer the question for the audience members—"What's in it for me?"

# 19

# *IMPROMPTU SPEAKING*

*It usually takes me three weeks to prepare a good impromptu speech.*
*— Mark Twain*

Impromptu speeches are delivered in "off the cuff" situations, such as at business meetings. You might be at a Rotary breakfast meeting when the president calls on you to give the group an update on your committee's work. Or, while you are at a department meeting, your supervisor may ask you to explain how you handled a troublesome situation.

In most cases, you will be speaking on a subject you already know about; you only need to organize your thoughts. You will do more impromptu speaking than any other kind, but because it's not planned, you might not think of it in terms of an actual speaking situation.

Impromptu speaking is sometimes viewed as more of a predicament than a method of delivery, especially when people naturally expect us to have the right words at the right time. Clergy may be invited to a luncheon or community dinner expecting to be part of the crowd when, with no notice, they are called on to give a short prayer. The human resources director may be hoping to mingle with employees at the company picnic, but if the CEO asks her to give an overview of the company, she'd better have the speaking skills to do so! In general, people ask you to speak about areas of your expertise. Otherwise, they wouldn't make the request.

Since an impromptu talk provides no advance notice, you are denied the advantage of preparation. Hence, impromptu speeches work best if you cover only one brief topic. Delivery is more casual than with a formal speech.

For example, spokespersons for airlines hastily assemble press conferences and speak extemporaneously when an airplane crashes. They may not have had the luxury to prepare their speeches, but they organize their thoughts as best they can under pressure.

While impromptu speeches are not formally prepared, you can take the techniques learned in preparing an informative or persuasive speech and use them in an off-the-cuff situation.

If there is any possibility, no matter how remote, that you may be asked to say a few words at a meeting or gathering, have your thoughts organized. It is better to be prepared and not be called on than not to be prepared. The worst thing that will happen is that you will spend a little preparation time on a speech and then not use it.

Most likely any impromptu presentation will concern a subject with which you are familiar, so you need only organize information and ideas you already possess.

## TAKE ADVANTAGE OF AN IMPROMPTU OPPORTUNITY

To take full advantage of an impromptu speaking opportunity, keep in mind four major points:

### 1. Use the Time between Being Asked and Actually Speaking to Your Benefit

An impromptu situation does not require a 15-minute talk. Scoring one sharp point can make you look like a real pro. When people ask you to talk, pause a second and think about the subject. Every presentation needs a beginning and an end, no matter how short the speech. The beginning could be short or elongated, depending on how much time you need to buy.

If you asked me, "What is your favorite season, and why?" I could just answer, "Spring," but that doesn't say anything about me or the reason for my choice. It would be better for me to say, "My favorite season is . . ." while I take a short time to collect my thoughts.

If I needed a little more time, I could say, "I have the advantage of living in the Northeast, where we have all four seasons, and each has its own special quality, but my favorite is . . ." I haven't said anything, but it has given me time, and it is better to take the time at the beginning than to begin stalling in the middle of your speech and put your audience off on a tangent. Listen to a presidential press conference, and you will see how a master politician stalls for time while collecting his thoughts to answer an unexpected question.

Review your personal experiences and use them. Do not be afraid to be original; you do not have to remember what every other expert says about your topic. If nothing else, consider the questions *who, what, when, where, how,* and devise a plan to answer one or more of them.

## 2. Observe What Is Going on Around You and Respond to It

If there are other speakers, you might comment on their points of view. You also can comment on the audience and the occasion, in addition to your topic. For example, "When I look around the room and see all the support, not only from politicians and public figures, but from parents, friends, and everyday people, I know that our battle with diabetes is going to be triumphant. I want to share with you where your contributions are going . . ."

## 3. Keep a Positive Attitude

People are not expecting perfection when you are speaking off the cuff. The audience realizes that you haven't had preparation time, so their expectations are low. Even so, do not put yourself down by saying, "Oh, I wasn't expecting to talk." Don't complain or object to speaking opportunities when you could be seizing them.

Think positive, and keep it simple. Simply give them a few pieces of evidence based on your experience—that's all they're asking you to tell them. Embellish it according to their particular needs.

### 4. Most Vital, Keep Your Comments Brief

If you have said everything you want to say or everything you can remember, wrap it up as neatly as possible and sit down. If you forgot something, it probably was not important anyway. If it was, the audience will ask you about it afterward.

Please, do not prolong your conclusion. While you do not want to stop abruptly and leave your audience up in the air without closure, you also don't want to ramble on, thinking you have not said enough, when the audience is thinking, "Why is he still talking? He's made his point." An impromptu speech can be one sentence long, as long as it has a beginning and end, and expresses one point very strongly.

## DELIVERING THE IMPROMPTU SPEECH

You want your speech to be an audience-centered, positive delivery. Consider, though, what typically happens. You are at a meeting, sitting at a table, and you are asked to talk. You've been making doodles on your agenda, and you are leaning to the left or right as you begin to speak. You speak only to the person who asked you the question. Do you look authoritative? No.

### Show Authority or Credibility

When you are asked to speak, use the same techniques that you would use in a speech. Stand when possible, otherwise sit up straight. When seated, you have to work a little harder to deliver your punches, so give your diaphragm some help and take a deep breath. Plant your feet firmly on the floor with your knees together and lean forward. This will help you to gesture and connect with your audience.

- Keep your chin up and smile as you make eye contact with everyone around the table.
- Look at people beside you without swiveling in your chair.
- Don't stare across the table or at the one person who asked the question.
- Share your eye contact.
- Increase your volume slightly, and pause for emphasis.

### Maintain Poise

In presenting an impromptu speech, your attitude is the deciding factor in determining your ultimate effectiveness. I cannot overemphasize the importance of poise. Do not fidget in your seat before you speak because you know you will soon be "on the spot." When you are called on and the situation lends you an opportunity to stand before the group, rise calmly and take your place before your audience.

If you speak from a podium, begin your remarks calmly, without hurrying, and with some vigor and force. Have a plan in mind to develop your thoughts. In your introduction, tell why the subject is important. When you begin to speak, do not make any apology whatsoever. Get on with your speech.

### Pick Up Speed and Power as You Go Along

In actually delivering an impromptu talk, it is wise not to start too fast but rather to pick up speed and power as you go along. Aside from this, observe bodily actions and gestures in keeping with the speech situation. Naturally, your articulation, pronunciation, and grammar should be of the highest standards.

There is little to fear from impromptu speaking if you follow a preconceived method of attack on your subject. Do not allow yourself to become panicky; some nervousness is a good sign of readiness. Realize that your audience will expect nothing extraordinary from you because they too know you are speaking impromptu. Actually, they will probably be pulling for you. If you go about your task with poise and determination, your chances of success are exceedingly good.

# 20

## HOW TO BE A BETTER LISTENER

*We have two ears and only
one tongue in order that
we may hear more and
speak less.*
— *Diogenes*

To speak to the needs of an audience, you have to hear the needs. To be a better listener, you have to first want to be one. In this brief chapter, we'll review some steps to help you improve your own listening.

### ACCEPT THE SPEAKER'S PECULIARITIES

This may be difficult to do. Take watching the evening news, for example. If you see Tom Brokaw or another familiar anchor, you tend to deemphasize the speaker's appearance. If the anchor is on vacation and there is a substitute, you may be distracted from listening to the news.

Female anchors present a special challenge because they vary their hair styles, the colors of their clothes, and their jewelry. Anything that is too exaggerated—too large a pin, too bright a shade of lipstick—can be easily distracting.

153

So, too, all speakers differ. Accepting distracting behavior and then focusing on the listening task will be difficult at first. Practice is essential.

## IMPROVE YOUR ATTITUDE

You have to develop a positive mental attitude to guide you into more effective listening. Instead of saying, "My attention span isn't what it used to be," or "I think sometimes my hearing isn't good," take positive action. If you have had family, friends, or business associates complain that you are not hearing what they are saying, then have your hearing checked to eliminate that as a possibility.

If your hearing is adequate, begin to work actively on your listening skills as outlined in this chapter. Do not accept the disempowering excuse that you are not a good listener. Do something about it.

## IMPROVE THE ENVIRONMENT

Select a position in the room that provides for a better listening environment. Stay away from entrances or exits; do not select a place too far away from the speaker. Do not sit next to a group that may be talking during the speech. When people enter a room, they tend to sit at the back. Change that habit. Take a front row seat, and see how your listening skills improve.

## WITHHOLD JUDGMENT

As you have seen in the chapter on persuasive speaking, one technique is to present the negatives of a view before the positive. If you are listening to such a speech, and begin to judge the speaker's content from the beginning, then you will miss the point of the speech.

Make an effort to be open-minded, especially if you think you might be hostile to the subject. Hold your judgment until the speaker is finished.

## IMPROVE YOUR NOTE TAKING

Many times when we listen to speeches, we feel compelled to copy the speakers' visuals or write their train of thought, as well as write our own ideas as they occur. Don't attempt to jot down every word. Taking detailed notes interferes with the listening process. Be flexible in patterning your notes.

You could try to outline the speech in the same way you would if you were preparing it: Look for the speaker's purpose, write down the three to five main points, and the person's closing statement.

## SELECT THE SPECIFIC LISTENING PURPOSE

Deciding why you are listening helps you focus your listening activity. Find your WIIFM. If you are at the presentation to pick up new information, then focus on gleaning that information. If you are at the presentation to weigh the pros and cons of buying a service or product, then listen for and list those pros and cons.

## USE TIME WISELY

You may not have realized it, but your listening speed is faster than your speaking speed. Therefore plan the use of the time differential. How many times have you found yourself listening intently to a speech, only to find a few seconds later that your mind has wandered? Daydreaming here can be an unwise use of spare time. Direct this time into review and anticipation of the speaker's new ideas. Channel this time into systems that help you understand or remember the speaker's ideas or concepts.

## LISTEN RATIONALLY

Emotional reaction can interfere with your listening. If you have ever sat in a doctor's office and heard news that would affect your life significantly, you know that the moments after hearing "your test was positive" are difficult ones to focus on hearing what the doctor says next.

Speeches that evoke an emotional reaction can have the same effect. If emotional reaction interferes with listening, recondition yourself to react less emotionally. Learn to delay the emotional reaction until after the communication. Focus on "understanding" rather than on "acceptance."

# MASTERING THE MECHANICS

## WHAT'S IN IT FOR YOU

Chapter 21 will help you to think ahead about everything you will need to make your presentation flow smoothly and trouble-free. Use the Speaking Aids Checklist so you never forget anything.

If you do not know how to use the room you are speaking in to its full advantage, you may be missing out. Reading Chapter 22 will raise your awareness about how to arrange seating to suit your audience's size and needs. Tips on mastering the microphone and making final checks for your visual aids will help you to create a comfortable audience. Use the Room Checklist to ensure you have covered everything.

How can visual aids help you make your point? Chapter 23 covers it. You'll know the types of visual aids and how to use each when you've completed this chapter. Use the checklist for constructing a visual aid at the end of the chapter and you will have useful visuals.

If you plan to present with a computer as a sidekick don't miss Chapter 24. Room checks for computers can be a lifesaver if you rely on a computer to make your point. Again, there is a checklist so you don't miss anything.

# SPEAKING AIDS

*Never rise till you have*
*something to say, and*
*when you have said it*
*cease.*
                    *—John Witherspoon*

**W**hatever your gender, there is one rule that we all learn as children, those of us in the Scouts anyway. *Be prepared!*

Preparing your speech is crucial. I've included a checklist for speech preparation in Chapter 25. Nevertheless, no matter how well you prepare your speech or how many times you practice it out loud, you won't be ready until you have made sure that all the accessories and equipment you need will be there and ready for your presentation.

Can you imagine planning your speech around the use of slides and then arriving at the site to find there is no slide projector? Since this kind of disaster is so easily prevented, there is no reason for it to happen.

The first thing to do is complete the checklist at the end of this chapter. Think ahead about everything you will need to make your presentation flow smoothly and trouble-free. Then ask your host or sponsor which items can be provided and which you bring yourself.

If the sponsor has a seating arrangement with names, ask for it in advance. When I have a seating chart available, I tape it to the lectern so I can call on people by name. Large tent cards with names written in dark ink are also helpful for this. People respond much better if you use their names when asking questions.

As a result of my own experiences as well as from hearing other speaker's horror stories, I always carry my presentation aids on the plane with me. It's a lot safer to take your slides out of the carousel and carry them in boxes with you than to risk their getting mixed up with luggage that's going to Pongo Pongo.

Although it's impractical to carry 150 copies of a bulky report with you, at least carry the original in case the copies get lost. You can always have more copies made right before the presentation.

On the day before the presentation, call the sponsor and double-check that all the equipment you requested is available. Also ask if the number of participants has increased or decreased. Attendance figures can fluctuate rapidly at the last minute.

## Hot Tips

- Look at the room prior to speaking.
- Get the phone number of the room or location.
- Have backup visual aids in case there is a problem with your originals.

# CHECKLIST: SPEAKING AIDS

*How Many*

- ☐ Note Pads          _____
- ☐ Pens/Pencils/Marking Pens/Chalk _____
- ☐ Chalk Board
- ☐ Flipchart Easel/Markers     _____
- ☐ Pointer
- ☐ Name Tags          _____
- ☐ Flipchart Pad        _____
- ☐ Overhead Projector
- ☐ Transparencies       _____
- ☐ Slides/Film/Videotape
  - _____ $^3/_4''$ VHS
  - _____ $^1/_2''$ VHS
  - _____ $^1/_2''$ BETA
- ☐ LCD Panel
- ☐ Slide Projector
  - _____ Automatic advance with Sound
  - _____ Manual advance without Sound
- ☐ Film Projector
- ☐ Videotape Player
  - _____ $^3/_4''$ Videotape Player
  - _____ $^1/_2''$ Videotape Player (VHS/BETA)
- ☐ TV Monitor
- ☐ Written Materials       *How Many*
  - _____ Reports    _____
  - _____ Material   _____
  - _____ Prereading _____
- ☐ Tape/Duct Tape
- ☐ Extra Bulbs
- ☐ Projection Screen
- ☐ Microphones
- ☐ Podium
- ☐ Extension Cords
- ☐ Refreshments (specify)

  _____
- ☐ Facilities
  - _____ Room _____ Seating Arrangement
  - _____ Room setup (diagram if necessary)

# 22

# *POINTERS FOR USING THE ROOM*

*We have forty million
reasons for failures, but
not a single excuse.*
　　　　*—Rudyard Kipling*

**W**hen you are to give a presentation, ideally you should have a say in how the room is set up so that the arrangement works best for you, and you should be able to check the room out before the scheduled time for your speech. Unfortunately, many of us walk into situations without those options.

If you fly in from out of town to give a speech in a conference room in your client's building, you may find yourself speaking in a room that doubles as a storage room and copier room, or you may be on a stage in a private and plush auditorium with spotlights and every kind of audiovisual equipment you could want.

One simple thing most people don't think about doing (unless you paid attention when you read the previous chapter) is phoning ahead to get details about the room and the equipment. Check with your client's secretary about the room you will be in, and if you want a pitcher of water and a microphone, ask for them.

The following sections highlight factors for your consideration if you have access to the room in which you will be speaking.

## ARRANGING SEATING TO SUIT YOU AND YOUR AUDIENCE

In preparing the room, sit in various areas to confirm that your visuals can be seen from every chair. Move chairs if you have to.

If you have a large audience and you do not mind a one-way situation with little interaction, then have the room set up in theater, classroom, or crescent shape.

This arrangement is the easiest for the speaker because your audience is all in one direction in front of you and your visual aids are beside or behind you. (See Figures 22.1 and 22.2.)

If your group is smaller, 25 people or less, and you want some interaction between people, then a U- or V-shaped seating arrangement works best. This arrangement still works fine for the speaker because you are in the opening at the end, and your visual aids are in the center. (See Figure 22.3.)

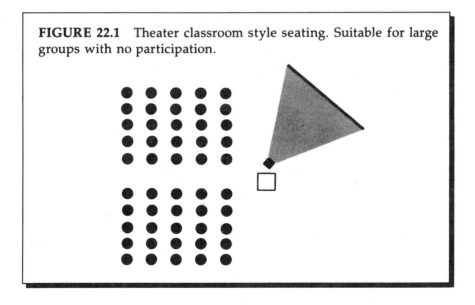

**FIGURE 22.1**   Theater classroom style seating. Suitable for large groups with no participation.

**FIGURE 22.2**   Crescent-shaped seating. Recommended for large audiences and for meetings that do not require workspace for the participants.

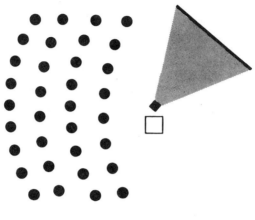

**FIGURE 22.3**   U- or V-shaped seating. Best for groups under 20 and for presentations that involve discussion and participation.

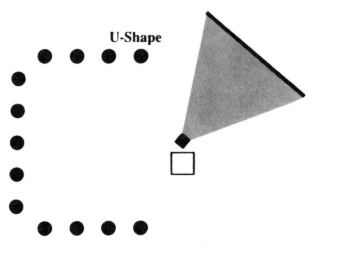

U-Shape

Another option is to have the speaker in the center and the visual aids in the opening at the end. It is not an ideal situation because you must take care not to block the view of your audience.

This arrangement is not good for audiences with more than 25 people because the shape becomes so wide that it is hard to look at the people in the corners as you speak.

For very small groups at a typical department meeting or in a boardroom, the circle or square seating arrangement works best:

This arrangement promotes interaction among the participants, but it is difficult for the speaker, who cranes her neck to speak directly to the people on either side of her, and any placement of visual aids is awkward for at least one fourth of the group.

In choosing your seating arrangement, you not only must consider the logistics of how many people you will be speaking to but also ask yourself, "What do I want to achieve?" and "What is going to work best for me?" The room needs to be large enough to be comfortable and uncluttered to make movement easy and obstacle free. Realize that there are options for you to set up the room both to suit your purpose and to accommodate the audience.

## CHECKING OUT YOUR SPEAKING AIDS

When possible, practice your presentation in the room where you will give it. That is the best way to check out the speaking aids you will use, as well as other equipment, such as the podium or the microphone.

Make sure the lectern or podium is placed where you want it to be, or removed if you don't wish to use it. I suggest that you speak without it. Historically, we used the podium because speeches were written out, the audience's attention span was much longer before the advent of commercial television, and often we spoke before much larger groups of people.

Think about what role the podium plays. It creates a barrier that separates you from your audience and gives speakers a crutch or a place to hide. Speaking is an audience-centered sport. You don't want to hold back your adrenalin and energy. If you step out from behind the podium, move toward your audience, and gesture, the actions provide a good release for you and allow you to hold the interest of your listeners a lot longer.

Visualize a speaker behind a podium. Doesn't the speaker seem removed, maybe even larger than life? You make yourself more accessible to your audience when you do not use the podium. Although you may feel vulnerable at first, you will find you have more rapport with the audience. It's worth the lack of protection! You can still leave your notes there. Just walk behind the podium to refer to them and then come in front again.

When he was on the campaign trail for the presidency, Michael Dukakis frequently ran into problems when speaking because of his height. The podium and microphone were often too tall for him and made him appear dwarfed when standing next to his Democratic opponents during the primaries. The best thing you can do is to practice speaking comfortably without a podium.

## MASTERING THE MICROPHONE

Because microphones are commonly mounted on podiums, you may not be able to dispense with the podium. However, the advent of wireless microphones is changing this situation. When you check the room arrangements, also check the room's acoustics.

If you need a microphone, see if a wireless mike is available. If you speak often, you may want to purchase your own. They are not expensive—Radio Shack carries one that is about $50.

I have one caution for you, based on the experience of a colleague named Barbara. She was leading a writing seminar for 50 people in a banquet room and was given a wireless microphone to use for the first time. She thought it was wonderful because she didn't have to worry about tripping over the cord, and she could walk freely up and down the aisles. After a couple of minutes, she forgot that she was even wearing the microphone.

The morning session went well; during break she fielded her participants' questions and then resumed the class. She gave the group a 5-minute writing exercise and left to go down the hall to the women's restroom. She had just relieved herself of her morning coffee when a woman burst into the bathroom and yelled, "Barbara, your mike is on!"

Barbara turned off her mike, and the woman asked her if she felt able to go back into the class, and she said, "Sure." To herself, she thought, "What in the world am I going to say to this group that I have basically gone to the bathroom in front of?" She walked down the hall, which had by that time become a very long hall, and walked into the class, where the group was laughing away.

"I have never used a remote mike before," she said. "And there is a whole school of thought that says you need to have a significant emotional experience to change behavior. I just had my significant emotional experience, and never again will I forget to turn off my mike."

Besides the wireless mike and the podium mike you could also choose among *lavaliere, clip-on, table,* or *floor* mikes:

- Lavaliere. Hangs around the neck allowing you good freedom of movement. Watch where you step to avoid the cord.

- Clip-on. Attaches to your lapel, tie, or other garment. Many lavaliere mikes also serve as clip-ons.

- Table. Rests in a holder that stands upright on a table. Allows for movement in front of or behind the table.

- Floor. Rests in a freestanding holder, can be placed anywhere in the room. Enhances audience participation.

## CHECKING OUT YOUR VISUAL AIDS

Arrive early at the room where you are speaking and check out the basic requirements for your visual aids.

---

**CHECKLIST: VISUAL AIDS**

☐ Find all electrical outlets and test them.

☐ Check the lighting and light switches.

☐ Make sure that you and the room are equipped with every-thing you need, from blackboard and chalk or flipcharts, to projection equipment.

☐ Carry an extra extension cord and spare light bulbs with you, if you can.

---

Then, set up your visual aids and check their visibility from various seats throughout the room. If some chairs have blocked views, move them. *Do not assume anything.*

You may know that your equipment works because you tested it at your office; but when you get ready to speak and start to plug in your projector, you may be caught off guard by a detail as small as a three-pronged cord not fitting into a two-pronged outlet.

## *ELIMINATING DISTRACTIONS*

It is difficult to predict what distractions might plague your speech, but if you stand in the room where you are to speak and look around, you might be able to brainstorm through a few. For example, if there is a telephone in the room, request that all phone calls be put on hold. If the phone is an extension, turn off the bell so that the phone will not ring in that room.

If your meeting is informal and participants will be getting up to get coffee or to enter and exit the room, make sure that the participant's chairs are arranged so that their backs are to the door or the coffee table.

If you are speaking in front of a window and the light from the window will be at your back, you probably want to pull the shades down, even if it is cloudy. A sudden flash of sunlight will strain your audience's eyes, make it hard to see the speaker when backlit, and interrupt the presentation of a visual aid.

If you can, find out who will be using adjacent rooms and what potential disturbances, if any, may arise.

## CREATING A COMFORTABLE ATMOSPHERE CONDUCIVE TO LEARNING

As discussed in Chapter 5, atmosphere counts! Room temperature or ventilation doesn't become an issue until it's too late and your audience is falling asleep or going outside to put on their coats. Check the air conditioning and ventilation systems for the room in which you will be speaking.

Most rooms have individual thermostats. If a lot of people are going to be in the room, you will want to drop the temperature to 65 degrees to compensate for the rise in temperature caused by the added body heat.

Since too much heat makes people tired, it is better to have people a little chilly than warm. Be especially careful of the temperature in the afternoon, when people are likely to be tired from lunch. Also, make sure that the room is well ventilated by a door, window, or fan. The more you can keep a normal flow of oxygen, the more alert your audience will be.

## UPDATING YOUR CHECKLIST

If you speak often, add to your checklist as you discover new items you need to inspect, such as the location of restrooms. You may think this detail unimportant, until you find yourself wandering around an old three-story municipal building with men's rooms at every turn, but no women's room in sight (or vice versa), and you have five minutes before you are scheduled to speak!

To close the chapter, here's a checklist to help you ensure that your room is all squared away:

**CHECKLIST: THE ROOM**

☐ Set up the room to suit your purpose and to accommodate the audience.

☐ Check that the room is large enough for comfort and easy movement.

☐ Practice your speech in the room where you'll give it.

☐ Place the lectern or podium in the proper place.

☐ Use a wireless microphone if a microphone is necessary.

☐ Check the room's acoustics.

☐ Arrive early to check out speaking and visual aids.

☐ Find all electrical outlets and test them.

☐ Check the lighting and light switches.

☐ Make sure you have all necessary equipment: blackboard and chalk or flipcharts, spare extension cord, light bulbs, projection equipment, etc.

☐ Check the visibility of all visuals from every seat in the room.

☐ Have phone calls put on hold.

☐ Place participants' chairs so their backs are to the door.

☐ Pull window shades if the speaker's place is in front of the window.

☐ Check the air conditioning and ventilation systems.

☐ Set the room temperature at six degrees below normal.

☐ Make sure the room has good ventilation.

Last, but never least, find out where the restrooms are.

# 23

## HOW VISUAL AIDS CAN HELP

*Visual Aids are no substitute for good basic speaking skills.*
*—John K. Borchardt*

**W**henever you have an opportunity to use visual aids in your presentations, use them. They enhance your message and facilitate a dramatic increase in your audience's retention rate. Do not let yourself be restricted by others who do not use visual aids. You lead the way. Use them, and teach others to follow your example. Paula George, CEO and founder of the SoftAd Group says, "Using slides, videos, or product demonstrations saves you a lot of tedious explaining and helps your audience get excited about your topic." Use visuals to enhance your own excitement about the points you are stressing.

People think in pictures. In your visual aids, use pictures instead of words where you can. When you think of a car what does your mind do? Create a picture or a word? Most people see a picture of a car, not the letters C-A-R. Retention is better when we see a picture along with the words.

Often the subject of a speech is complicated. Perhaps you are describing a new sales promotion plan, an organizational blueprint, or tactics for solving a problem. It would seem natural to use a visual aid to help the listener grasp the complete idea while keeping track of the individual parts.

With visual aids, the audience can see what is being discussed, whether the aid is a graphic design, a list of words, or a sketch.

The speaker also benefits from visual aids. They allow you to move physically and with purpose and give you something to do. As a result, you will do a better job of speaking. They also can remind the speaker what to say and when to say it. They help to relieve tension and create interest.

A major caution is to use visual aids for only one purpose: to enhance your presentation. They are never the presentation itself. Use them, but in moderation:

- Give your audience a chance to look over the visual aid before you begin talking about it.
- Talk to your audience, not the visual aid.
- Practice using your visual aids at least once so that you are comfortable working with them in front of your audience.

## *TYPES OF VISUALS*

A visual can be the written word on a handout or transparency, a two-dimensional picture on a slide, or a three-dimensional figure in a videotape or in a model. You can choose among many types of visual aids for your presentation.

For example, if you were going to give a persuasive speech to an uninformed audience, you might want to show a five-minute videotape to provide your audience with an overview of your subject. While video tapes can accomplish a great deal in a small amount of time, they are very expensive to produce.

The most commonly available visual aids are flipcharts, handouts, overhead projection, and slides. Within the next 5 years, the most common will be computer-screened overheads that you can design on the spot to look polished and professional. Before deciding which type of visual aid to use in your presentation, first consider your audience and the purpose of your speech. Then check the following visual aid profiles to determine which type is best.

## Videotapes

Videotapes can be movies, demonstrations, or training films.

If you plan to use a videotape, preview it first. Know how to use the video equipment before you begin. Explain to the group what they will be seeing and give them specifics to watch for. If the video lasts more than 20 minutes, stop the tape to debrief the key sections. Keep lights on in the room so it is not dark. Make sure your viewing monitor is large enough so everyone in the room can see.

## Flipcharts

A flipchart is a large pad of white paper mounted on an easel. It is bound at the top and hangs loose at the bottom so that as you fill a page, using a magic marker, you can flip that page to the back of the easel and start writing on a new page.

Flipcharts are best used in small, informal group settings, such as training sessions, when you want to encourage interaction. As with a chalkboard, you can write as you speak or make up your flipchart in advance. If your audience brings up new ideas, you have the flexibility of adding those ideas to your chart.

The main disadvantage of a flipchart is that you may spend considerable time writing on it and not facing your audience. A flipchart can also be sloppy and awkward, especially when you are flipping through the entire pad to find something that you wrote earlier.

Blue and black are the best colors to use on flipcharts because the dense colors show up well. You can use several colors for variety or emphasis, but never use red and green together—they show no contrast when viewed by a color-blind person, and color blindness is more common than you think.

Colors have meaning. When you assign appropriate colors to your messages you will be most effective; for example, the color red is associated with stopping and attention. The color green represents growth. Which color would you use to highlight your sales figures for next year?

Use two blank sheets of chart paper between each of your written pages to avoid bleeding ink or shadows from the pages beneath. Mr. Sketch brand markers do not bleed and have a pleasant smell. Do not use dryboard markers, they have a toxic odor that makes some people sick—me included. Also, check your flipchart easel for stability before you begin pressing down to write on the paper.

As for page layout, follow a few simple rules for visibility. Print in letters that are at least two to three inches high and use a combination of upper- and lower-case letters. Two- to three-inch margins on either side are best, with the bottom margin about one fourth of the page.

Follow the "4 times 4" rule—use no more than four lines and four words per line on any flipchart page. Use a headline and bullet the key points so that anyone in the audience who loses your attention will have a point of reference to get back on track.

I knew a professional trainer who, at first glance, had beautiful flipcharts, but in the context of a presentation, they were poor quality. These charts were written in gold-lettered calligraphy, with at least 50 words on each page. When you use visual aids, take the time to learn to use them correctly or they will detract from your presentation.

You want to keep control of where the audience is looking, so stand close to your flipchart. Stand next to your visual so the audience can look at you and the visual at the same time. If you are right-handed, then stand to the left as you write. You don't want to block the pad as you write or point across your body when referring to it.

If you made your flipchart in advance, stay to the right of the easel and touch where you want the audience to look. That is the first of the three T's—touch, turn, and talk—as you use a

**CHECKLIST: TIPS FOR USING FLIPCHARTS**

☐ Letters or numbers should be two to four inches tall.

☐ Follow the 4 × 4 Rule.

☐ Only use top three-fourths of page.

☐ Write in two to four colors.

☐ 3M correction tape can cover up a mistake.

☐ Staple your pages together so you can find your place in them easily, and use strips of clean paper to cover words you don't want your audience to see yet, and to help you build to a point.

☐ If you know that people cannot see your visual aid from a certain section of the room, remove the chairs from that section before your audience arrives.

☐ When you finish using the flipchart, turn to a clean page, or put the easel to the side of the room where your chart will not be a distraction during the remainder of your speech.

☐ Turn up the bottom corner of the page for ease in turning.

visual aid. You want to speak to your audience, not your visual aid, so after you touch your key point, turn to the audience, establish eye contact with someone, and continue to talk. Don't cross your hand over your body to touch the visual; rather, use the hand closest to the flipchart.

## OVERHEAD PROJECTION

Overhead projection requires a piece of equipment called an overhead projector, plus markers and clear plastic sheets or transparencies. You lay these transparencies, one at a time, on the glass surface of the projector, lit by a bulb, and a lens projects the image of your words onto a screen or blank wall. Transparencies need to be made up in advance. You may use overlays to develop your points one phrase at a time.

Overhead projection is an inexpensive visual aid that can project images large enough to be seen by a large group or small enough to be used for a more intimate gathering. Overhead projection is being used in business and technical presentations, congressional hearing rooms, and classrooms.

The main disadvantage of overhead transparencies is that they are so easy to use that they are often abused. Too many people put their entire presentations on the transparencies. Listening to a song once can be pleasurable. If you have to listen to the same song 10 times in a row the music will become annoying. Imagine eating 10 chocolates in a row. Even to the chocoholic, the tenth chocolate does not have the same appeal as the first.

Overdoing overheads has the same effect. If you use a visual aid to enhance every point of your presentation, then no key points will stand out.

When you design your transparencies, use colored markers to create emphasis or use color transparencies. If you type, use a simple typeface that is no smaller than 18 points for visibility (regular type is 10 points). As a test, put your transparency on the floor, and if you can read it while standing, then the typeface is large enough.

With transparencies, follow the "6 times 6" rule: Use no more than six lines and six words on any given line. Strive to stay in the center of the transparency to maintain proper margins around it. Also, don't use the bottom one fourth of the page. Tape your transparencies to frames to keep them from sticking together or slipping off when you pick them up. A frame cuts down on the noise of the plastic as well. I've found "flip frames," a 3M product, to be superior. You slide each transparency into a frame that you can write notes on. The envelopes also protect the transparencies from fingerprints. They can be stored in a three-ring binder.

The only time to stand at the overhead projector is when writing, in which case you would be using a very high screen, so your head does not block the audience's view. Otherwise, stand to the side of the screen and use a pointer. Remember to touch, turn, and talk to your audience. If you don't need your pointer, put it away. The pointer is not a toy. Don't wave, conduct, duel, fondle, or continually contract the pointer. Do put the pointer on a table or podium when it is not in use.

Number your transparencies and place them in sequence in a box or large envelope for protection. Mark the order of use on the outline of your speech and make a separate index of your transparencies.

Every overhead projector is different. You will want to arrive early and turn the machine on to adjust it. Check the neck of the machine to make sure it projects high enough on the wall so that your audience can see the screen. Carry an extension cord in case you have to move the machine. Also, in case the light bulb in the machine burns out, carry extra bulbs and learn how to change them.

Finally, when you finish using the machine as part of your presentation, turn it off and move away so that it does not become a distraction to the audience.

## SLIDES

Slides can be made on your computer. Slides are an excellent visual aid for formal presentations and large groups.

Create your slides with a dark background and light print. This will allow you to keep the lights on during your presentation. Don't turn off all the lights; people will get sleepy.

Limit the number of slides you use, and keep the wording on each slide brief and simple. It is easy to enhance slides to the point of overkill. Some speakers are enamored by all the bells and whistles that computer graphics can now add to their visuals. Their slides are so detailed that audience members cannot retain the one simple key point.

With slides, in general, stand at the front of the room and face your audience. The slides are a tool—not the presentation. To change the slides, use a remote control. To avoid confusion about which button goes forward, put a piece of masking tape on your forward button—it will feel different and you'll know you are pushing the right button. To give a complete slide presentation, dim the lights to remove any distractions from the screen. If you are merely using a few slides to enhance your oral presentation, then keep the lights on. If the room is dim, use a lighted pointer. Practice with it first!

Before your audience arrives, check the order of your slides and run them through the projector to make sure that none are upside down or backward. A speaker with upside-down slides seems disorganized and careless regardless of how well the rest of the presentation is going. As with the overhead projector, carry an extension cord and extra light bulbs just in case, and know how to change the bulb.

When you have finished with your visual aid, turn the slide projector off and if the lights were dimmed, signal for them to be turned up again. Put your lighted pointer away, so that all distractions of your visual aids are now gone.

## HANDOUTS

Handouts are typed pages pertaining to your subject that you copy and distribute to your audience. Handouts are a good idea for any presentation that covers a subject so broad that you cannot put it all into your speech. Handouts may be an outline of your key points that allows your audience to follow along and either take notes or not take notes because you have the pertinent information down on paper.

Handouts may give an overview of the company you represent, or explain the features of the product or service you are trying to sell. They are intended to enhance your speech, so don't overwhelm your audience with an avalanche of papers to sort through and carry home.

You can distribute handouts before your presentation, during your presentation at the breaking points, or after your presentation is over. Always tell your audience about the intended use of the information. Emphasize that you will make references to the handouts.

When designing, make sure your handouts are numbered and leave room for notes.

Avoid distributing the handouts while speaking, unless it is an informal and intimate group of five or less. Keep the attention on yourself as speaker, not on the handouts. You want to make eye contact with your audience, not talk to a room full of people who have their heads down while reading their handouts.

## THE MAKING OF A GOOD VISUAL AID

Each one of these visual aids can serve a significant purpose for the speaker and the listener. However, visual aids need to be planned, constructed, and used wisely. The effective speaker knows his visual aids and handles them smoothly. This takes practice, but the results are worth it.

Potentially good visual aids are often wasted. To avoid this:

- Keep visual aids simple.
- Make sure your lettering is large and easily seen.
- Write neatly (because your visual aids are a reflection on you).
- Always check your spelling.
- Limit the number to your key points.

## THE CONTENT OF VISUAL AIDS

Your audience and your topic will determine which type of written visual aid is best. The first type of listing emphasizes the main points of your speech. For example, a visual aid using main points:

> Advertising Plan for European Motors
> Television Auto Special
> Motor Journal Road Tests
> National Auto Show

You could also use numbers or statistics that are important to your presentation. For example, a visual aid using statistics:

| | |
|---|---|
| Materials Up | 9% |
| Labor Up | 3% |
| Advertising Up | 7% |
| Shipping Down | 1% |

Depending on your topic, you may also want to list the names of persons, places, or things. For example, a visual aid using names:

> Comparative Classes of American vs. Foreign Cars
> Low-Priced:   Ford vs. Volkswagen
> Mid-Priced:   Pontiac vs. Honda
> High-Priced:  Cadillac vs. Mercedes Benz

### Graphs and Charts

Graphic visual aids are simply constructed charts or geometric designs offering a compact view of specific items in relation to the whole. They help the audience to make easy comparisons, see changes, or grasp the entire picture.

The line graph permits the audience to see at a glance the increases and decreases occurring over a period of time (see Figure 23.1). It instantly illustrates what otherwise would require much time and effort to explain. The line graph improves listener understanding and aids recall of the information.

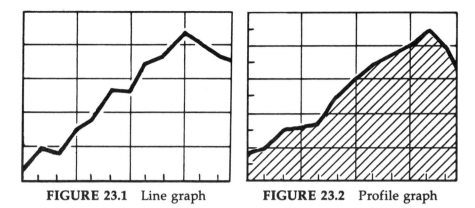

**FIGURE 23.1** Line graph   **FIGURE 23.2** Profile graph

The profile graph is similar to the line graph (see Figure 23.2). The only difference is in the use of shading beneath the data line. Although both types of graphs convey the same visual information, the profile is recommended as a variation when showing large or significant changes in data in relation to specific intervals. It helps your audience concentrate on such special fluctuations.

The bar graph has the advantage of presenting your audience with blocks of information in a form allowing visual comparison (see Figure 23.3). Unlike the line graph, the bar graph condenses data not needed to be shown in exact detail, thereby quickly achieving listener understanding.

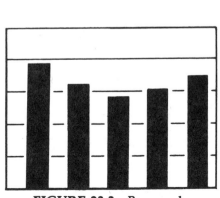

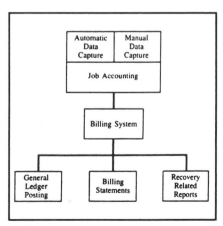

**FIGURE 23.3** Bar graph   **FIGURE 23.4** Organization chart

Organization charts are especially important when you are discussing a complex subject consisting of many divisions of influence (see Figure 23.4). Whether the subject is a political group or procedure, a business complex or a chain-of-command, or even the local social group, this particular visual aid is essential for the listener who is trying to assemble the pieces in the organizational jigsaw.

The pie chart has a rather unique characteristic (see Figure 23.5). It clearly illustrates the divisions or pieces in relation to one another while remaining within the visual setting of the whole. Your audience is shown a combination of elements and also can compare their relationships.

Like the written visual aid, graphics can be sketched on a blackboard either during the speech or before it. However, if the graphic aid is especially complicated, it is advisable to construct it before the presentation. The advantage of the graph is that your audience can clearly and easily see the relationship of the parts to the whole and can, therefore, find greater meaning in your presentation.

The pictograph shows the same type of information as other graphs but uses a representative figure rather than a line or bar

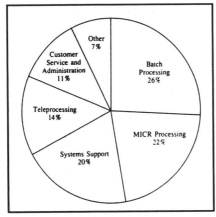

**FIGURE 23.5**   Pie chart

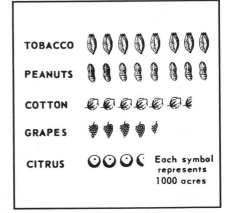

**Figure 23.6**   Pictograph

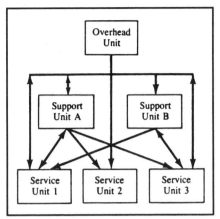

**FIGURE 23.7** Flow chart

(see Figure 23.6). This graph can be used to highlight certain features of a presentation.

The flow chart is a visual aid that shows viewers a series of sequences or relationships (see Figure 23.7).

Simply because you took the time to prepare visual aids, your audience will be able to see information and hear about it simultaneously, thereby doubling their impression. As a result, you will be considered a better speaker.

---

**CHECKLIST: CONSTRUCTING A VISUAL AID**

☐ Make the entire visual aid twice as large as may seem necessary.

☐ Use printed letters rather than script (keep the visual aid neat).

☐ Print or draw with heavy dark lines.

☐ Use two or more simple visual aids, rather than one complicated one.

☐ Use a maximum of five colors.

☐ Keep it simple.

☐ Offer one key point per visual aid.

☐ Double-check spelling.

☐ Write in upper and lower case or all lower case.

☐ Use only the top three fourths of the page (for flipcharts).

☐ Practice using visuals several times before going live.

# 24

# ROOM CHECKS FOR COMPUTERS

*A PC on every desk and in*
*every home . . .*
*—William Gates,*
*Founder of Microsoft*

**A** s with any other equipment used as a visual aid to enhance
your presentation, if you are using a personal computer, take
the time to check the room setup before your scheduled speech
and run through your entire demonstration on site. A poorly
planned computer demonstration is damaging, especially if your
speech was meant to persuade your audience or to introduce a
new technology.

The following checklist of important details will help you create a
powerful computer-assisted presentation:

## PREPARE YOUR SOFTWARE CAREFULLY

Take the time to check out your demonstration software carefully
before the day of your presentation. Have an objective person
double-check spelling in all demonstration software, especially
the customer's name and product. Then:

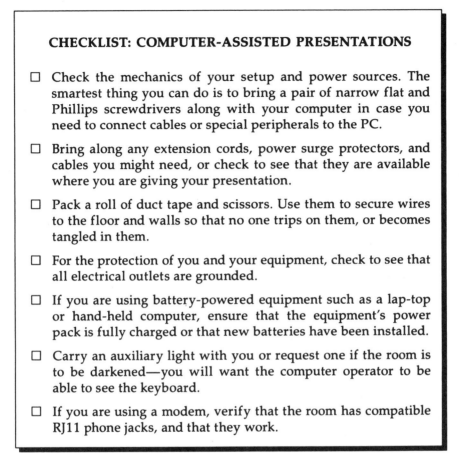

**CHECKLIST: COMPUTER-ASSISTED PRESENTATIONS**

☐ Check the mechanics of your setup and power sources. The smartest thing you can do is to bring a pair of narrow flat and Phillips screwdrivers along with your computer in case you need to connect cables or special peripherals to the PC.

☐ Bring along any extension cords, power surge protectors, and cables you might need, or check to see that they are available where you are giving your presentation.

☐ Pack a roll of duct tape and scissors. Use them to secure wires to the floor and walls so that no one trips on them, or becomes tangled in them.

☐ For the protection of you and your equipment, check to see that all electrical outlets are grounded.

☐ If you are using battery-powered equipment such as a lap-top or hand-held computer, ensure that the equipment's power pack is fully charged or that new batteries have been installed.

☐ Carry an auxiliary light with you or request one if the room is to be darkened—you will want the computer operator to be able to see the keyboard.

☐ If you are using a modem, verify that the room has compatible RJ11 phone jacks, and that they work.

- Prepare duplicate copies of the software and check it on your equipment.
- Bring duplicate copies of software with you.

Beware of working with rented or borrowed equipment. It is always best to work with your own equipment because you are familiar with it. If you have to rent equipment, see that it arrives early at the place of your presentation. Request that someone at the demonstration site receive it personally and have it delivered to the proper place of your presentation.

If you are using your client's equipment at the customer's site, test it in advance. Whenever you are using someone else's equipment, check its compatibility with your software.

## PREPARE FOR GOOD VISIBILITY

Once you are on the presentation site, check that the computer screen is visible to every seat. If you are projecting the computer screen image on a screen mounted to the wall, test to see that all colors show up and that there is a contrast between letters, graphics, and the background.

## SMOOTHING OUT YOUR PRESENTATION

Finally, to ensure a smooth presentation, run through the entire demonstration on-site if possible. When presenting a team demonstration, make sure the person operating the keyboard knows when to advance the software. Do not let anyone who does not know your system or software operate the keyboard.

The more you prepare and practice, the smoother you can make your presentation using computers as a visual aid.

## CHECKLIST: COMPUTER SETUP

☐ Check the room setup.

☐ If possible, practice the whole demonstration on-site.

☐ Bring the tools you need to set up and repair your equipment.

☐ Check that all extension cords, power surge protectors, and cables needed are available.

☐ Bring duct tape and scissors to secure wires to floor and walls.

☐ Make sure that all electrical outlets are grounded.

☐ If using battery-powered equipment such as a lap-top or hand-held computer, make sure power pack is fully charged or new batteries have been installed.

☐ If the room is to be darkened, see that the keyboard operator has an auxiliary light.

☐ If using a modem, make sure RJ11 phone jacks are in the room and that they work.

☐ Check spelling in all demo software, especially the customer's name and product.

☐ Bring duplicate copies of software.

☐ If renting equipment, make sure it arrives early and that someone at the demo site will receive it and have it delivered to the proper place.

☐ If using equipment at a customer's site, try it out in advance. If using someone else's equipment, check for compatibility.

☐ Check to see that the terminal is visible from every seat.

☐ If projecting the computer screen image on a large screen, make sure all colors show up and that there is a contrast between the background and the letters and graphics.

☐ If you are doing a team demonstration, coordinate your presentation in advance so that the person operating the keyboard knows when to advance the software.

☐ Finally, do not let anyone who does not know your system or software operate the keyboard. Treat it as your sacred turf.

# CHECKLISTS

## WHAT'S IN IT FOR YOU

Chapter 25 outlines the material in this book in a checklist format that you can use as a reminder before every presentation. After you have mastered the art of presenting, the checklist will reinforce what you have learned.

Finally, Chapter 26, "Speech Delivery Checklist," capsulizes the visual, vocal, and verbal information previously covered, and concludes with Guidelines for Superior Q&A Sessions.

# 25

# *SPEECH PREPARATION CHECKLIST*

*Luck is the meeting of
opportunity and
preparation.*
*— Anthony Robbins*

The checklist on pages 192 to 194 provides an outline of the previous chapters of this book. Use it as a reminder before every speech. The more you use the checklist, the sooner these steps will become second nature.

## CHECKLIST PREPARATION

- ☐ Know your purpose (to inform, persuade, or entertain).
- ☐ Know your audience (their attitudes, needs, demographics).
- ☐ Know the logistics (time of day, whether speaking alone or as a team).
- ☐ Limit your topic.
- ☐ Brainstorm for ideas on your topic.
- ☐ Select an appropriate method or organization.
- ☐ Outline your 3 to 5 main points: (80 percent of your presentation)
  - ☐ Remember the 75 percent rule of thumb.
  - ☐ Prepare for 1-hour speech as if you had only 45 minutes.
- ☐ Gather supporting information:
  - ☐ Current, accurate material, relative to topic.
  - ☐ Facts, statistics, examples, testimony, humor.
- ☐ Check for accuracy.
- ☐ Design your introduction: (10 to 15 percent of your presentation)
  - ☐ Grab the attention of your audience.
  - ☐ Establish WIIFM (what's in it for me).
  - ☐ Establish yourself as a credible source.
  - ☐ Preview your topic.
- ☐ Write your conclusion: (5 to 10 percent of your presentation)
  - ☐ It should be 5 to 10 percent of your presentation.
  - ☐ Review key points.
  - ☐ Make a memorable statement.

## FINAL DRAFT

☐ Use standard paper, not note cards:
- ☐ Type your outline in bold 14-point type or write in felt-tip black or blue pen.
- ☐ Use only on the top two thirds of the page.

☐ Write your introduction, transitions, and conclusion in phrases:
- ☐ Don't be too short or too long.
- ☐ Don't be too general.
- ☐ Don't overstructure.

☐ Indicate where you will use your visuals.

☐ Write grabber and memorable statement.

☐ Box material that can be eliminated if you run short on time.

☐ Make several copies of your final draft.

## VISUAL AIDS

☐ Select the type of visual that will be appropriate for your purpose and use only to reinforce or enhance your points.

☐ Use a variety of aids for interest:
- ☐ Flipcharts.
- ☐ Overhead projection transparencies.
- ☐ Computers.
- ☐ Videotape.
- ☐ Slides.
- ☐ Handouts.

☐ Have large, simple, clear, neat visual aids.

☐ Use colors for impact.

☐ Check the spelling.

## PRACTICE

- ☐ Deliver your speech out loud 3 to 6 times.
    - ☐ Practice in the room where you will speak, if possible.
    - ☐ Use your visual aids.
- ☐ Tape-record your speech and listen to it.

## BEFORE DELIVERY

- ☐ Arrive early.
- ☐ Bring extra bulbs, extension cords, tools for equipment.
- ☐ Check on room arrangements, acoustics, room temperature.
- ☐ Check room's acoustics; use a wireless microphone if available.
- ☐ Set up your visual aids:
    - ☐ Test electrical outlets, light switches.
    - ☐ Make sure you have everything you need—chalk, projection equipment, etc.
    - ☐ Check visibility of your visuals from every seat.
    - ☐ Check to see that slides are in order.
- ☐ Do body warm-ups:
    - ☐ Stretching exercises.
    - ☐ Deep breathing exercises.
    - ☐ Positive imagery.
- ☐ Check your appearance (be professional).
- ☐ Know your place on the agenda.

# 26

# SPEECH DELIVERY CHECKLIST

The two most difficult parts of public speaking are the wait just before your presentation and the very beginning of your presentation. If you know your topic and are sure that your beginning and end are good—because that's where you pull your audience in and where you leave them—then you should feel comfortable and secure.

Do your breathing exercises and come to the front of the room with purpose. Look for a familiar face in your audience and acknowledge anyone you know. You are nervous, but those butterflies are anticipation, energy, and excitement.

Whenever you are in a high-energy situation, you are going to feel adrenalin pumping. The first words out of your mouth are going to be good, because you practiced them and you know them.

You also know that your speech is audience-centered. Whether you are addressing your peers or your supervisors, you have information that they need. You wouldn't be there giving the presentation if you didn't. Evaluate your audience, know the situation, and make sure you present the information so that it is understandable.

The following checklist outlines the information covered in previous chapters:

## VISUAL SKILLS

### Approaching the Podium

- ☐ Dress to support, not hinder, your speech.
- ☐ Step up to speak with confidence and authority.
- ☐ Arrange your outline and visuals before starting to speak.
- ☐ Stand up straight yet relaxed; don't lean.
- ☐ Smile.
- ☐ Establish eye contact with your audience before speaking.
- ☐ Begin your speech without referring to your notes.

### Eye Communication

- ☐ Make eye contact with your audience; focus on each person 3 to 5 seconds; finish your thought.
- ☐ Don't look at the floor or out the window.
- ☐ Refer to your outline only occasionally.

### Body Language

- ☐ Use your face to add interest and look confident.
- ☐ Keep your chin up.
- ☐ Appear to enjoy speaking.
- ☐ Gesture effectively:
    - ☐ Open palms.
    - ☐ Vary motions.
    - ☐ Keep gestures visible, smooth, natural, and reinforcing.
    - ☐ Keep hands up and out, broad and flowing.
- ☐ Move intentionally:
    - ☐ Move away from the podium to get close to your audience.
    - ☐ Don't pace.
    - ☐ When stationary, keep your feet still; do not dance, or shift, or cross legs.

**Attention**

- ☐ Care that your audience listens.
- ☐ Do not distract your audience by playing with pens, pointers, jewelry, hair, clothes.
- ☐ Do not pack up early.

**Leaving the Podium**

- ☐ On finishing, move out with confidence.

## VISUAL AIDS

- ☐ Visual aids are another aspect of "nonverbals."
- ☐ Arrange visuals so they can be seen from every seat in the room.
- ☐ Keep them covered until you are ready to use them.
- ☐ Introduce visuals when pertinent.
- ☐ Use visual aids to enhance the message, not be the message.
- ☐ Focus attention on your audience, not the visual aids.

## VOCAL SKILLS

- ☐ Speak with enthusiasm.
- ☐ Sound interested.
- ☐ Sound sincere.
- ☐ Sound extemporaneous, not as though reading or reciting.
- ☐ Keep your pitch comfortably low and vary it.
- ☐ Speak at 125 to 150 words per minute:
  - ☐ Vary the rate.
  - ☐ Do not speak too fast or too slow.
  - ☐ Vary the volume of your voice.
  - ☐ Speak loud enough to be heard.

☐ Pronounce your words correctly:

    ☐ Do not cut off the ends of words, such as "ing."

    ☐ Enunciate clearly.

    ☐ Avoid "uh," "um," "you know," or giggling.

☐ Use pauses effectively.

☐ Stop at the end of an idea.

    ☐ Do not hook sentences together with "and" or "and uh."

    ☐ Drop pitch, not volume, at the end of sentences.

    ☐ Do not use a rising intonation at the end of sentences.

☐ Hide, do not emphasize, your goofs.

☐ Speak with, not at, the audience.

## VERBAL SKILLS

☐ Be descriptive.

☐ Start with your grabber statement to spark interest and create a need.

☐ Use transitions to make the presentation flow.

☐ Make your information interesting, useful, and understandable.

☐ Reiterate your information to enhance retention.

☐ Avoid words that create doubt, such as—*kind of, sort of, I hope, I guess, perhaps.*

☐ Time your speech accurately.

## GUIDELINES FOR SUPERIOR Q&A SESSIONS

☐ Encourage questions from your audience.

☐ Repeat or paraphrase the question.

☐ Be brief.

☐ Be honest.

☐ Be prepared.

☐ If you do not know the answer to a question, do not lie.

☐ Get rid of stage hogs fast.

☐ If you anticipate hostile questions, set up guidelines:

    ☐ Do not engage in a battle.

    ☐ Let the person vent his or her anger.

    ☐ Paraphrase what the person just said.

    ☐ Ask the person a question.

    ☐ Either refute the person's view or problem solve.

☐ End the question-and-answer session with a closing statement.

The only way you can improve your delivery is to practice again and again, while noting your mistakes. Tape-record yourself, go over each point, concentrate on any weak areas, and listen to your revisions. Then tape your actual performance, or have a friend rate you for objectivity on all the points.

# A FINAL WORD
## Improving Your Personal Speaking Style

As you move from your first presentation to the point where you lose count of how many times you have addressed audiences, remember the simple truth stated earlier: More people have talked their way up the ladder of success than have gotten there any other way.

Communication skills are valuable tools; it is up to you to practice and develop them. Here are some suggestions for continually adding to your presentation skills:

---

**CHECKLIST FOR DEVELOPING PRESENTATION SKILLS**

☐ Speak at every opportunity.

☐ Observe able speakers and learn from them.

☐ Read good literature.

☐ Use a dictionary and thesaurus to strengthen your vocabulary.

☐ Practice writing.

☐ Rehearse your talks with a tape recorder and a critical listener.

☐ Listen to recordings and studio videotapes of great speakers.

---

There is no standard measure of the length of your speech—whether it is informative, persuasive, or impromptu. You can watch a 30-second commercial on television and be sold on a product. On the other hand, you can sit for hours and listen to a sales presentation and not feel like buying.

After 45 minutes, generally it gets hard to sit and listen to anyone speak, so you are more effective with a shorter presentation. It is always better to think in terms of your audience and your content, and to ask yourself: "Have I said what I wanted to say?"

# BIBLIOGRAPHY

*Stand Up, Speak Out, and Win.* Keith DeGreen (Ed.), Cincinnati: Summit Enterprises, 1977.

*Change Your Voice, Change Your Life.* Morton Cooper, New York: Macmillan, 1984.

*Before You Say a Word.* Myles Martel, PhD, Englewood Cliffs, NJ: Prentice-Hall, 1984.

*Speaking to Groups: Eyeball to Eyeball.* James B. Anderson, Vienna, VA: Wyndamoor Press, 1989.

*Power Presentations on the Business Stage.* Nathelie Donnet, Toronto: Carswell Publications, 1988.

*Think on Your Feet.* Kenneth Wydrow, Englewood Cliffs, NJ: Prentice-Hall, 1981.

*Power Speak.* Dorothy Leeds, New York: Berkley Books.

*The Language of Love.* Gary Smalley and John Trent, Focus on the Family Publishing.

*Person to Person.* Elizabeth Jeffries, Louisville, KY: Leadership Press, 1986.

*The Heart of Leadership.* Elizabeth Jeffries, Louisville, KY: Leadership Press, 1990.

*Awaken the Giant Within.* Anthony Robbins, New York: Summit Books.

*The Seven Habits of Highly Effective People.* Stephen R. Covey, New York: Simon and Schuster, 1989.

## Newsletters

*The Executive Speaker.* Box 292437, Dayton, OH 45429, (513) 294-8493. Monthly.

You may contact the authors at the following addresses:

Marjorie Brody
Brody Communications
1200 Melrose Avenue
Melrose Park, PA 19126

Shawn Kent
Kent Associates
547 Astor Square
West Chester, PA 19380

# INDEX